Intermediate 1

MW01697954

STECK-VAUGHN

TEST BEST®

Stanford

Tenth Edition

ISBN 0-7398-8803-X

Printed in the United States of America.

3 4 5 6 7 8 9 10 030 10 09 08 07 06 05

Harcourt Achieve

Rigby • Steck-Vaughn

www.HarcourtAchieve.com

1.800.531.5015

Table of Contents

Data, Statistics, and Probability

Geometry and Measurement

PRACTICE POSTTEST FOR STANFORD 10
Test Battery, Intermediate 1 Level

Test Materials

Mathematics Problem Solving

DIRECTIONS ▶

Read each question or problem carefully. Then answer the question or work the problem. Mark the space for your answer.

SAMPLE A

What is the value of the 5 in this number?

1853

A 5 ones
B 5 tens
C 5 hundreds
D 5 thousands

SAMPLE B

The chart shows the lengths of four U.S. bridges.

Four U.S. Bridges

Name	Length (in meters)
Golden Gate	1280
George Washington	1067
Tacoma Narrows II	853
Mackinac	2626

Which bridge is the *shortest*?

A Golden Gate
B George Washington
C Tacoma Narrows II
D Mackinac

1

The city of Calgary, Alberta, in Canada had a population of 821,628 in 1996. What is 821,628 rounded to the nearest thousand?

A 800,000
B 820,000
C 822,000
D 821,600

2

Greece has an area of 50,961 square miles. What is the value of 9 in 50,961?

A 9000
B 900
C 90
D 9

3

For a timed run in gym class, Gabriel ran a distance of 1.35 miles, Gina ran 0.78 miles, Leah ran 1.68 miles, and Tony ran 0.94 miles. Who ran the *greatest* distance?

A Gabriel
B Gina
C Leah
D Tony

4

Which clues could be used to describe the number 64?

A It is an odd number that is a multiple of 9.

B It is an even number that is a multiple of 6.

C It is an odd number that can be divided evenly by 5.

D It is an even number that can be divided evenly by 4.

5

Malcolm has seventeen hundred coins in his collection. How is that written as a number?

A 17

B 170

C 1700

D 17,000

6

The Wilderness Club gives a flashlight to each new member. Each flashlight needs two batteries. Batteries are sold in packages of 8 batteries. The club buys 14 packages of batteries.

How many flashlights will the club have batteries for?

A 56

B 70

C 84

D 112

7

Arnold is saving to buy a new bicycle helmet and a bicycle seat. The helmet costs $19.95. He has saved $23.75. What other information is needed to find how much more money Arnold needs to save?

A The amount Arnold earns each week

B The cost of the bicycle helmet

C The cost of the bicycle seat

D The amount Arnold saves each week

8

Tent Peak in the Himalayan Mountains is 24,165 feet high. Another mountain in the Himalayas is about 4000 feet higher than Tent Peak. What height is 4000 feet higher than 24,165 feet?

A 24,169 feet
B 28,165 feet
C 28,565 feet
D 64,165 feet

9

If $Q + 19 = 41$, which of the following must be true?

A $Q = 41 - 19$
B $Q = 19 - 41$
C $Q = 41 \div 19$
D $Q = 41 \times 19$

10

Terrence collected 191 soda cans for recycling and Harriet collected 308 cans. *About* how many cans did they collect in all?

A 200
B 300
C 500
D 800

11

Which number goes in the □ to make the number sentence true?

$$\square \times 1 = 219$$

A 219
B 218
C 29
D 1

12

Mr. Riley is buying muffins for a meeting at his office. He sees 6 packages of muffins in the bakery case. Each package of muffins has 4 muffins in it.

What is a fast way for Mr. Riley to find out how many muffins are in all 6 packages?

A 6×4
B 6×5
C $6 + 4$
D $6 + 5$

13

Jason, Jorge, Michael, and Abdul are all reading a book for school. Jason has read $\frac{5}{10}$ of the book, Jorge has read $\frac{4}{10}$, Michael has read $\frac{8}{10}$, and Abdul has read $\frac{10}{10}$. Who has read the *smallest* fraction of the book?

A Jason

B Jorge

C Michael

D Abdul

14

Ms. Ramirez has a box of 96 crayons to give out to the 18 students in her class. Each student will get the same number of crayons. Which statement is *true*?

A Each student gets fewer than 2 crayons.

B Each student gets fewer than 3 crayons.

C Each student gets more than 4 crayons.

D Each student gets more than 7 crayons.

15

The chart shows the number of students in several schools.

Students in School

School	Number of Students
Lincoln Elementary School	1154
North Lake Middle School	1768
Cedar Middle School	1853
Roosevelt High School	2591

What number sentence could be used to find out how many more students go to Roosevelt High School than North Lake Middle School?

A $2591 + 1768 = \square$

B $1768 - 2591 = \square$

C $2591 - 1768 = \square$

D $2591 \div 1768 = \square$

16

Brandy, Lauren, Margo, and Allison sold boxes of Wilderness Girls cookies. Brandy sold the most boxes of cookies. Lauren sold 5 boxes less than Brandy. Margo sold 10 boxes less than Lauren. Allison sold 5 boxes less than Margo. Which of the following *could* be true?

A Allison sold 15 more boxes than Lauren.

B Lauren sold 10 more boxes than Allison.

C Brandy sold 20 more boxes than Allison.

D Margo sold 5 more boxes than Brandy.

17

The Howser Building is twice as tall as the Triangle Tower Building. The Triangle Tower Building is 12 stories taller than the Midtown Hotel. The Midtown Hotel is 5 stories shorter than the Washington Hotel. If the Washington Hotel is 20 stories tall, how tall is the Howser Building?

A 27 stories

B 54 stories

C 57 stories

D 74 stories

18

Maris has 12 large squares of colored cloth that are each the same size. Six squares are purple and 6 squares are red. She needs 48 small squares to make a design for the edge of a quilt.

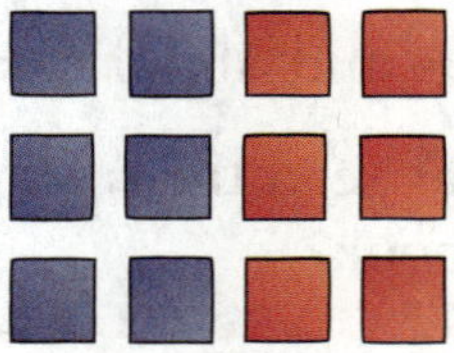

What could Maris do to make the 12 large squares into 48 small squares?

A Cut each square in half

B Cut each square into fourths

C Cut the purple squares into thirds

D Cut the red squares into fifths

19

Phillip's dog just had puppies.

What fractional part of all the puppies is black?

A $\frac{1}{6}$

B $\frac{1}{5}$

C $\frac{2}{6}$

D $\frac{3}{6}$

20

The chart shows the lengths of some rivers.

Lengths of Rivers

River	Length (in miles)
Yukon River	1979
Platte River	990
Pecos River	926
Canadian River	906
Tennessee-French Broad River	886
Yellowstone River	692

Which river is between 910 and 985 miles long?

A Yukon River
B Canadian River
C Pecos River
D Platte River

21

Over the summer, Travis read 25 books. He read 8 books about dinosaurs, 6 books about airplanes, and some books about trains. How many books about trains did Travis read?

A 19
B 17
C 14
D 11

22

Sami's school is raising money for new sports supplies. In the past, the school has sold several different products to raise money.

Products Sold

Product	Amount Raised
Wrapping paper	$10,256.00
Popcorn	$5268.00
Coffee	$7659.00
Candles	$4600.00
Flower seeds	$6471.00
Magazine subscriptions	$4385.00

Which products have earned the school *more* than $7000.00?

A Coffee and Popcorn
B Wrapping paper and Coffee
C Candles and Magazine subscriptions
D Flower seeds and Popcorn

23

On vacation, the Gillis family drove 276 miles on Sunday. Then they drove 318 miles on Wednesday. To return home, they drove 495 miles on Saturday.

About how many miles did the Gillis family drive on vacation altogether?

A 1100 miles
B 1000 miles
C 900 miles
D 800 miles

24

Su-Ming worked this problem on paper.

$$345 + 89 = \square$$

How could Su-Ming know that her answer is wrong?

A The answer should have 4 digits.

B The answer should be less than 89.

C The answer should be more than 345.

D The answer should have 1 as the middle digit.

25

Sarah is training for a long bicycle race. She starts by riding 15 miles during the first week. Her training schedule follows the pattern shown in the chart below.

Sarah's Training Schedule

Week	Number of Miles to Ride
1	15
2	21
3	27
4	33
5	39
6	45
7	?

If Sarah continues this pattern, how many miles will she ride in Week 7?

A 48

B 51

C 54

D 56

26

Which tile could be used to create the following pattern?

A

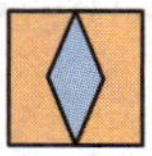

C

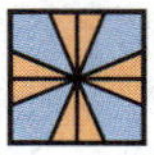

B

D

27

If $84 = b - 12$, what is the value of b?

A 96

C 72

B 92

D 7

28

Katherine is decorating a picture frame. She repeats the same pattern around the edge of the frame.

What figure is missing from Katherine's pattern?

A

C

B

D

29

Molly is painting the rooms in her house. She paints 2 rooms in 6 hours.

At this rate, how long will it take Molly to paint 7 rooms?

A 12 hours

B 15 hours

C 18 hours

D 21 hours

30

For Terry's birthday, he brings 30 cookies to share with the class. Each student takes one cookie on his or her turn. How many cookies will be left after the ninth person takes a cookie?

A 9

B 21

C 31

D 39

31

Julian's older brother has a job after school. The graph shows the amount of money Julian's brother earned at his after-school job each week for 6 weeks.

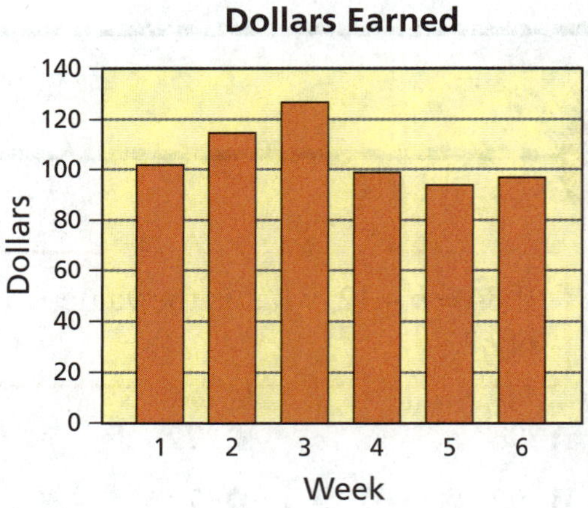

About how much did Julian's brother earn in week 3?

A $100

B $115

C $120

D $130

32

Mrs. Chu takes a pen out of the drawer. There are 3 red pens, 4 black pens, 5 blue pens, and 1 green pen.

If she chooses a pen without looking, what is the probability that she will choose a black pen?

A $\frac{4}{13}$ C $\frac{9}{13}$ B $\frac{4}{9}$ D $\frac{9}{4}$

33

Look at this spinner.

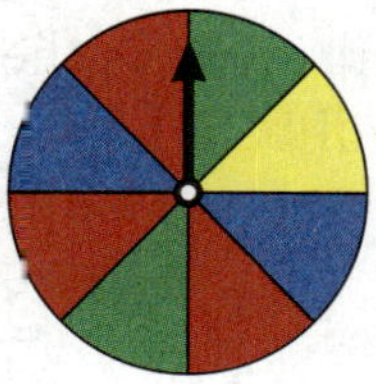

On what color is the arrow *most* likely to land if Tina spins it one time?

A Yellow **C** Blue

B Green **D** Red

34

The chart shows the favorite ice cream flavor of 90 people.

Favorite Ice Cream Flavors

Flavor	Number of People
Vanilla	11
Strawberry	13
Chocolate	26
Coffee	18
Rocky Road	22

How many more people chose chocolate or coffee than chose vanilla or rocky road?

A 4

B 7

C 11

D 15

35

Teri plans to exercise one hour a day. The chart shows the number of calories burned during one hour of exercise.

Calories Burned During Exercise

Activity	Calories Burned
Bicycling at 5 m.p.h.	174
Swimming	288
Walking at 2 m.p.h.	198
Tennis	312
Basketball	450
Walking at 3 m.p.h.	294

Which statement is *true* according to the chart?

A Teri can burn more than 200 calories by bicycling at 5 m.p.h. for one hour.

B Teri can burn more than 200 calories by walking 3 m.p.h. for one hour.

C Swimming burns more calories than playing tennis.

D Playing tennis burns more calories than playing basketball.

36

The chart shows the number of points earned by the Olympic gold-medal winners in a track-and-field event for the past few Summer Olympics.

Winning Points

Year	Number of Points
1996	8824
1992	8611
1988	8488
1984	8798

How many more points did the 1996 winner score than the 1988 winner?

A 26

B 213

C 310

D 336

37

Ms. Albert's class has 12 girls and 14 boys. If one student is chosen to feed the fish in the class aquarium, what is the probability that it will be a boy?

A $\frac{14}{12}$

B $\frac{14}{26}$

C $\frac{12}{14}$

D $\frac{26}{14}$

38

Yaakov places the following shapes in a bag and asks Daphne to draw out three without looking.

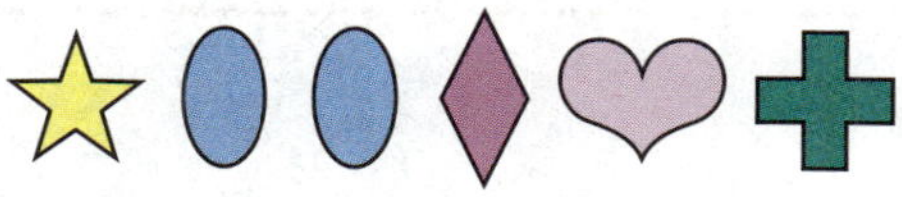

What combination of shapes would it be possible for Daphne to choose?

A

C

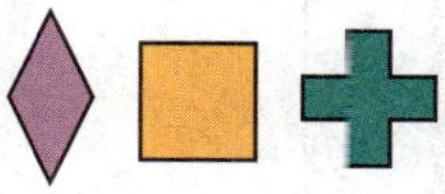

B

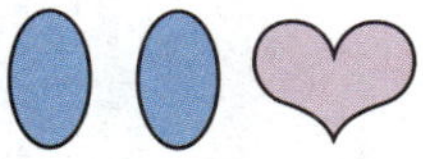

D

39

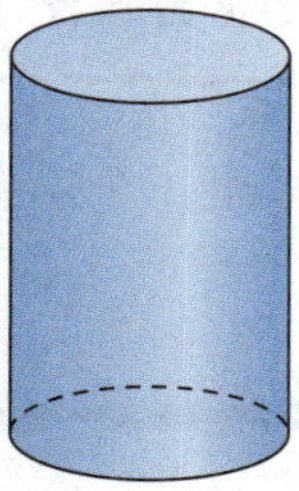

What is the name of the three-dimensional figure shown above?

A Cylinder

B Cone

C Circle

D Sphere

40

The map below shows the trails in Mountain Ridge State Park.

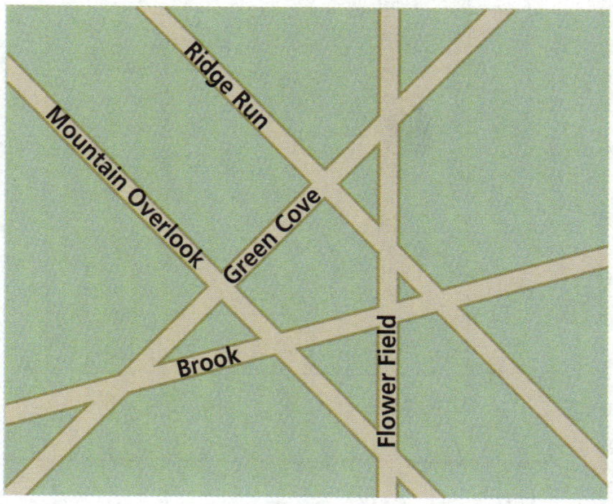

Which trail is perpendicular to Ridge Run Trail?

A Green Cove Trail

B Mountain Overlook Trail

C Brook Trail

D Flower Field Trail

41

Which measure could be the height of a grown man?

A 6 yards

B 6 inches

C 6 feet

D 6 square feet

42

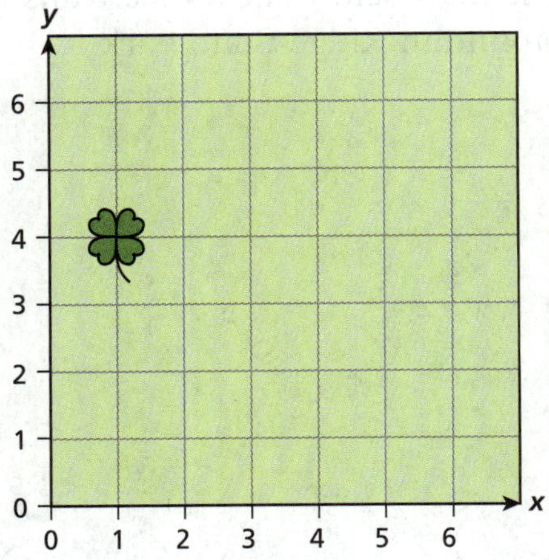

What pair of numbers shows the location of the four-leaf clover?

A (1, 1)
B (1, 4)
C (4, 1)
D (4, 4)

43

Which pattern could be folded to make a box?

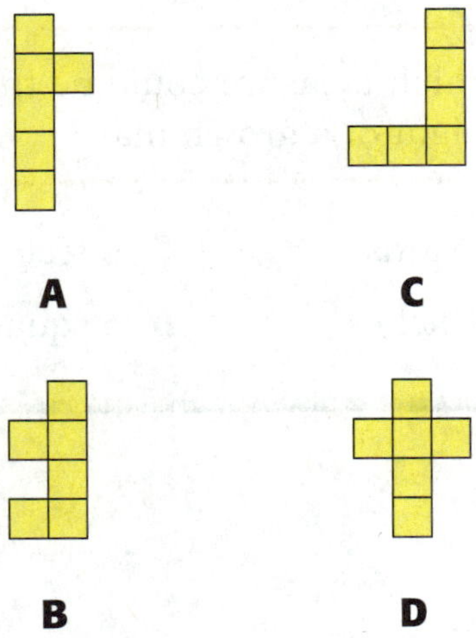

44

Ingrid has 67 cents. What is the *most* number of nickels she could have?

A 10
B 11
C 12
D 13

45

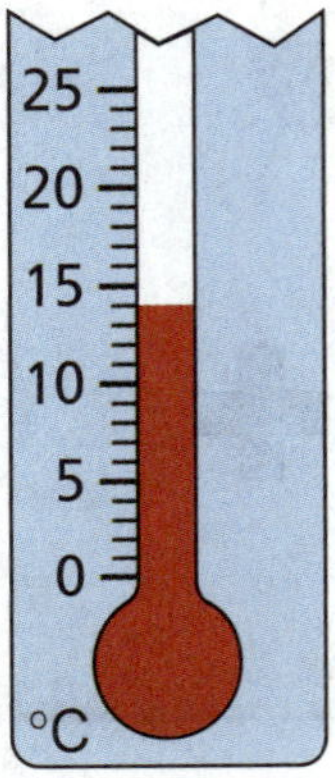

Which is the *best* estimate in degrees Celsius of the temperature shown on the thermometer?

A 10 °C
B 15 °C
C 20 °C
D 25 °C

46

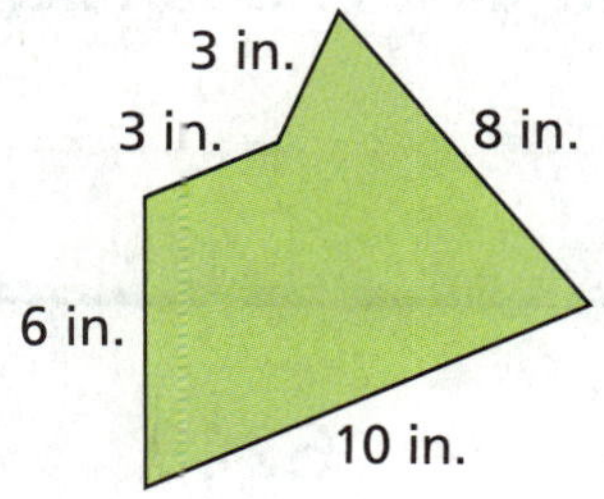

What is the perimeter of this figure in inches?

A 26 inches
B 28 inches
C 30 inches
D 33 inches

47

The school day is over at 3:00 P.M. Four students arrived home at the times shown in the table.

Name	Arrival Time at Home
Amanda	3:30 P.M.
Rashad	5:15 P.M.
Lu Duc	4:05 P.M.
Darlene	4:45 P.M.

Which student took the longest time to arrive home?

A Amanda
B Lu Duc
C Darlene
D Rashad

48

Use your inch ruler to help you answer this question.

Shane drew a map of the route he took on his bicycle ride Saturday. His ride started and ended at his home.

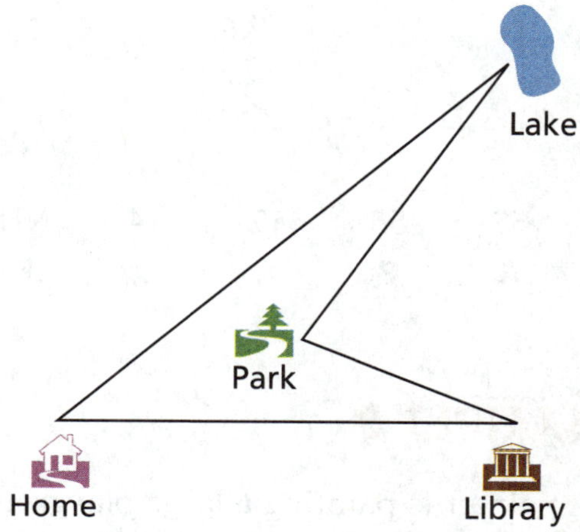

How many inches long is the route on Shane's map?

A 6 in.
B 7 in.
C 8 in.
D 9 in.

DIRECTIONS

Read each question or problem carefully. Then answer the question or work the problem. Mark the space for your answer. If a correct answer is *not here*, mark the space for NH.

SAMPLE A

$$\begin{array}{r} 36 \\ -\ 21 \\ \hline \end{array}$$

57	55	17	14	NH
A	**B**	**C**	**D**	**E**

SAMPLE B

A painter is painting a large playground. The painter will use 38 gallons of blue paint and 24 gallons of orange paint.

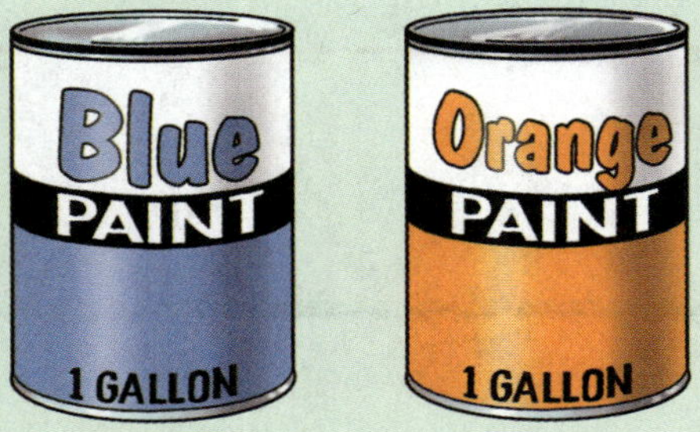

38 Gallons   24 Gallons

How many gallons of paint will the painter use in all?

A 14 gallons
B 52 gallons
C 62 gallons
D 64 gallons
E NH

1

$$\begin{array}{r} 6749 \\ +\ 414 \\ \hline \end{array}$$

7153	7163	7263	8153	NH
A	**B**	**C**	**D**	**E**

2

$$\begin{array}{r} 8.73 \\ +\ 1.58 \\ \hline \end{array}$$

11.31	10.41	10.31	9.41	NH
A	**B**	**C**	**D**	**E**

3

$$\begin{array}{r} 1284 \\ -\ 548 \\ \hline \end{array}$$

632	636	732	836	NH
A	**B**	**C**	**D**	**E**

4

$2.36 - 1.59 = \square$

A	B	C	D	E
0.77	0.86	0.87	1.77	NH

5

$$\begin{array}{r} 113 \\ \times\ 56 \\ \hline \end{array}$$

A	B	C	D	E
5338	6228	6328	6338	NH

6

$\frac{3}{11} + \frac{6}{11} = \square$

A	B	C	D	E
$\frac{3}{22}$	$\frac{3}{11}$	$\frac{9}{22}$	$\frac{9}{11}$	$\frac{14}{17}$

7

$\frac{4}{7} - \frac{2}{7} = \square$

A	B	C	D	E
$\frac{2}{14}$	$\frac{2}{7}$	$\frac{4}{14}$	$\frac{6}{14}$	$\frac{2}{0}$

8

$56 \div 8 = \square$

A	B	C	D	E
6	7	8	9	NH

9

$$\begin{array}{r} 4318 \\ +\ 757 \\ \hline \end{array}$$

A	B	C	D	E
4065	4075	5065	5075	NH

10

$$\begin{array}{r} 342 \\ -\ 199 \\ \hline \end{array}$$

A	B	C	D	E
42	43	142	243	NH

11

$$\begin{array}{r} 56 \\ \times\ 40 \\ \hline \end{array}$$

A	B	C	D	E
2260	2240	2040	224	NH

12

$53 \div 8 = \square$

A	B	C	D	E
6	6 R5	7	7 R3	NH

13

$8 \times 4 = \square$

A	B	C	D	E
24	28	32	36	NH

14

$13.20 - 5.33 = \square$

A	B	C	D	E
7.87	7.97	8.67	8.87	NH

15

$\frac{6}{9} + \frac{2}{9} = \square$

A	B	C	D	E
$\frac{4}{18}$	$\frac{4}{9}$	$\frac{8}{18}$	$\frac{8}{9}$	$\frac{15}{18}$

16

$\frac{9}{15} - \frac{5}{15} = \square$

A	B	C	D	E
$\frac{4}{30}$	$\frac{4}{15}$	$\frac{4}{0}$	$\frac{14}{30}$	$\frac{14}{15}$

17

Yuri is mailing three boxes of books. The first box weighs 24 pounds, the second weighs 43 pounds, and the third weighs 37 pounds.

What is the total weight of the boxes?

A 94 pounds
B 102 pounds
C 104 pounds
D 112 pounds
E NH

18

Shweta is ordering a DVD on the Internet. The DVD costs $14.99. The shipping charge is $4.50.

INVOICE

ITEM	PRICE
1 DVD	$14.99
SHIPPING CHARGE	$4.50

What is the total cost of the DVD, including the shipping charge?

A $19.49

B $18.99

C $17.99

D $16.49

E NH

19

Lucy and Jim ordered a pizza. Jim ate $\frac{5}{8}$ of the pizza. Lucy ate $\frac{3}{8}$ of the pizza.

How much more pizza did Jim eat than Lucy?

$\frac{1}{8}$	$\frac{2}{8}$	$\frac{3}{8}$	$\frac{5}{8}$	$\frac{8}{8}$
A	**B**	**C**	**D**	**E**

20

Janine spent $42.00 on three CDs. The three CDs each cost the same amount.

$42.00

How much did each CD cost?

A $12.00

B $13.00

C $14.00

D $15.00

E NH

21

Brian is baking muffins for the school bake sale. Brian has 6 packages of muffin mix to prepare. Each package of muffin mix makes 12 muffins.

6 packages

How many muffins will Brian make using all 6 boxes of muffin mix?

A 18

B 24

C 60

D 84

E NH

22

The class craft project is building birdhouses. Each birdhouse kit has 7 pieces of wood. There are 20 students in the class and each student has a complete kit.

7 p eces of wood

How many total pieces of wood does the class have?

A 100

B 120

C 140

D 160

E NH

23

The population of Greenville is 1438. The population of Johnson City is 582 people.

How many more people live in Greenville than Johnson City?

A 856

B 866

C 956

D 976

E NH

24

Carmen is making a fruit salad. She has 1.1 pounds of strawberries, 1.35 pounds of grapes, and 0.85 pound of blueberries.

What is the total weight in pounds of the fruit in Carmen's salad?

A 3.3
B 2.3
C 2.2
D 3.2
E 3.0

25

Miguel saved $65.72 from his after-school job. He then spent $41.99 on a birthday gift for his mother.

How much money does Miguel have left?

$24.73	$23.73	$23.63	$22.63	NH
A	**B**	**C**	**D**	**E**

26

Marilee weeded $\frac{2}{5}$ of the garden on Monday afternoon and $\frac{1}{5}$ on Tuesday.

How much of the garden has Marilee weeded?

$\frac{1}{5}$	$\frac{3}{5}$	$\frac{3}{10}$	$\frac{1}{10}$	$\frac{2}{5}$
A	**B**	**C**	**D**	**E**

27

Jason and Merry are joggers. During the week, together they jogged a total of 42 miles. Jason and Merry each jogged the same number of miles.

How many miles did Jason and Merry each jog?

A 21

B 22

C 23

D 24

E NH

28

There are 14 teams in the basketball playoffs. Each team has 8 players.

14 Teams

8 Players

How many players are in the playoffs altogether?

A 104

B 108

C 112

D 114

E NH

29

The Perez family are running errands. They drive 3.6 miles to the grocery store, then 4.78 miles to the hardware store. Then they drive 8.41 miles to visit the park, and finally 5.6 miles to return home.

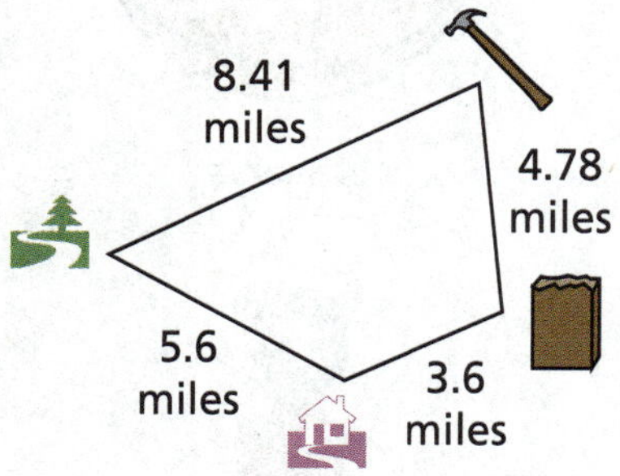

What is the total distance, in miles, that the Perez family drove?

A 19.39

B 20.39

C 21.39

D 22.39

E NH

30

The Screaming Eagle roller coaster has a drop of 147 feet. The Wild Ride roller coaster has a drop of 225 feet.

How many more feet is the drop on the Wild Ride than the drop on the Screaming Eagle?

A 372

B 122

C 78

D 22

E NH

31

Jeremiah chooses $\frac{4}{11}$ of his toys to put in a garage sale and gives $\frac{2}{11}$ to his little sister.

How much *greater* is the fraction of toys Jeremiah chose for the garage sale than the fraction he gave to his sister?

$\frac{2}{11}$	$\frac{2}{0}$	$\frac{6}{11}$	$\frac{6}{22}$	$\frac{8}{11}$
A	**B**	**C**	**D**	**E**

32

Last month, the bakery used 171.2 pounds of sugar. This month the bakery used 153.8 pounds of sugar.

How many more pounds of sugar did the bakery use last month than this month?

A 27.4

B 18.4

C 17.4

D 14.4

E NH

Skill FOCUS

Number Sense and Operations

Identify Place Value

Remember

Digits are the numerals 0, 1, 2, 3, 4, 5, 6, 7, 8, and 9.

Each digit in a number has *place value*. The value of a digit depends on its place in the number.

Any number can be written in a place-value chart. For example, look at the number 47,819 in a place-value chart.

ten thousands	thousands	hundreds	tens	ones
4	7	8	1	9

The number 4 in 47,819 has a value of 4 ten-thousands, or $4 \times 10{,}000 = 40{,}000$.

The number 7 has a value of 7 thousands, or $7 \times 1000 = 7000$.

The number 8 has a value of 8 hundreds, or $8 \times 100 = 800$.

The number 1 has a value of 1 ten, or $1 \times 10 = 10$.

The number 9 has a value of 9 ones, or $9 \times 1 = 9$.

So 47,819 is equal to $(4 \times 10{,}000) + (7 \times 1000) + (8 \times 100) + (1 \times 10) + (9 \times 1)$.

HINT

Base-ten blocks represent groups of one, ten, and one hundred.

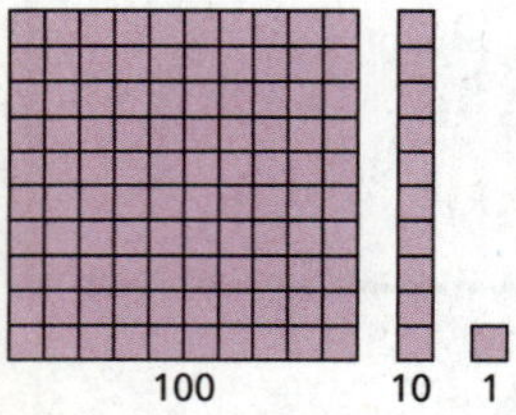

Another way to show place value is with base-ten blocks.

Look at the number 246 modeled with base-ten blocks.

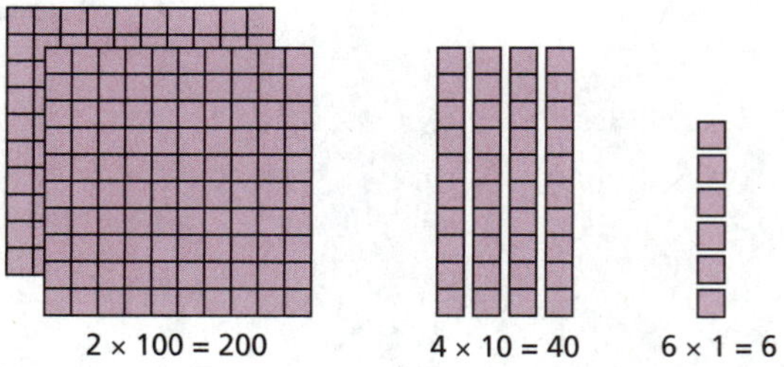

The 2 in the number 246 is in the hundreds place. It has a value of $2 \times 100 = 200$. The 4 in the tens place has a value of $4 \times 10 = 40$. The 6 in the ones place has a value of $6 \times 1 = 6$.

HINT

Here is a tip on how to regroup.

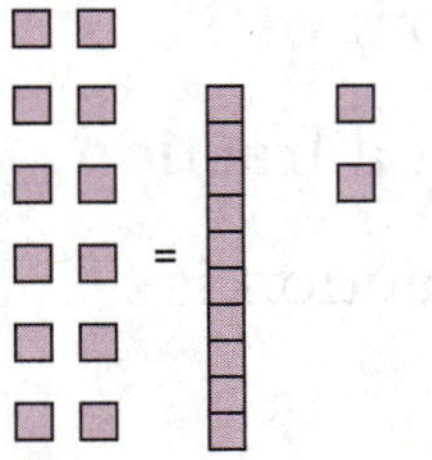

12 ones = 1 ten 2 ones

Each place value in a number can have only one digit. When working a problem, place values sometimes have to be *regrouped*, or ordered differently. For example, add the numbers 17 and 9. Adding the ones gives 16 ones. 16 ones = 1 ten + 6 ones. Write the 6 in the ones place for the total, and regroup the 1 ten to the tens place. 1 ten + 1 ten = 10 + 10 = 20.
So 19 + 7 = 2 tens + 6 ones = 26.

Example

Write the number represented by these base-ten blocks in a place-value chart. Remember to regroup.

____

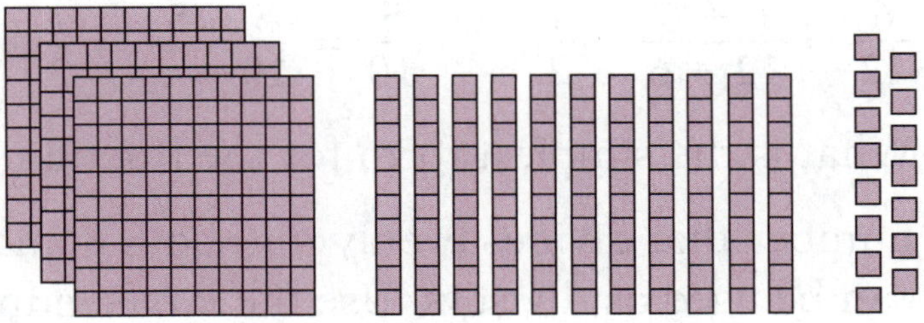

You could write the number in a place-value chart like this, but you must regroup.

Hundreds	Tens	Ones
3	11	15

First regroup the ones. 15 equals 1 ten plus 5 ones. So, write a 5 in the ones place for the answer. There are now 11 tens plus the regrouped ten. 12 tens equals 1 hundred plus 2 tens, or 100 + 20. Write a 2 in the tens place. Add the regrouped 1 hundred to the 3 hundreds, for 100 + 300 = 400. Write a 4 in the hundreds place for the answer.

Hundreds	Tens	Ones
4	2	5

Number Sense and Operations

Represent Numbers: Fractions

A *fraction* names a part of a whole.

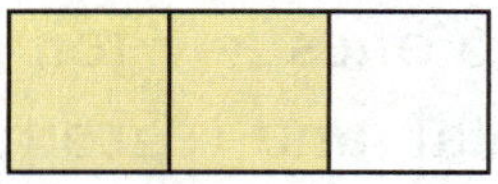

This rectangle is divided into 3 equal parts. 2 out of 3 parts are shaded. "2 out of 3" can be written as the fraction $\frac{2}{3}$. The top number of a fraction is called the *numerator*. The bottom number of a fraction is called the *denominator*.

> **Remember**
> The *numerator* is the top number of a fraction.
> The *denominator* is the bottom number of a fraction.

Simplest Form of a Fraction The fractions $\frac{6}{12}$, $\frac{5}{10}$, $\frac{3}{6}$, and $\frac{1}{2}$ are all equal to one another: $\frac{6}{12} = \frac{5}{10} = \frac{3}{6} = \frac{1}{2}$. The fraction $\frac{1}{2}$ is the *simplest form* of the fraction. A fraction is in its simplest form when no other number except 1 can divide the numerator and denominator evenly.

$$\frac{6}{12} = \frac{6 \div 6}{12 \div 6} = \frac{1}{2} \qquad \frac{5}{10} = \frac{5 \div 5}{10 \div 5} = \frac{1}{2} \qquad \frac{3}{6} = \frac{3 \div 3}{6 \div 3} = \frac{1}{2}$$

What is the simplest form for the fraction $\frac{8}{12}$? First, find a number that divides evenly into both 8 and 12. Both 2 and 4 can be used as divisors. Use the larger number as the divisor.

> **Remember**
> Multiplying or dividing the numerator and denominator by the same nonzero number does not change the value of the fraction.

$$\frac{8}{12} = \frac{8 \div 4}{12 \div 4} = \frac{2}{3}$$

Since no number except 1 can divide evenly into both 2 and 3, $\frac{2}{3}$ is the simplest form of $\frac{8}{12}$.

Improper Fractions and Mixed Numbers An *improper fraction* is a fraction whose numerator is greater than its denominator. Rewrite improper fractions as mixed numbers. A *mixed number* is a value represented by a whole number and a fraction.

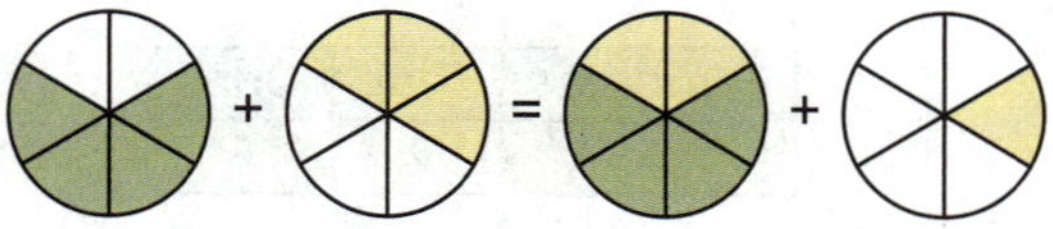

$$\frac{4}{6} + \frac{3}{6} = \frac{4+3}{6} = \frac{7}{6}$$

To write an improper fraction as a mixed number, divide the numerator by the denominator. The whole number in the quotient is the whole part of the mixed number. The remainder is placed over the divisor as the fraction part of the mixed number.

Since $7 \div 6 = 1R1$, $\frac{7}{6} = 1\frac{1}{6}$.

Example

What fraction of the circles is shaded? Write the answer in simplest form.

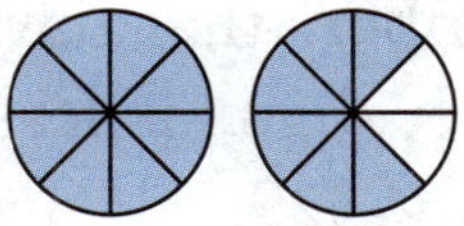

____

Each circle is divided into 8 equal parts. One whole circle is shaded, so the fraction of the circle that is shaded is $\frac{8}{8}$.

There are 6 shaded parts in the second circle. This means $\frac{6}{8}$ of the second circle is shaded. The circles represent the number $\frac{8}{8} + \frac{6}{8} = 1\frac{6}{8}$.

Write $\frac{6}{8}$ in simplest form.

Both 6 and 8 have a common factor of 2.

To write $\frac{6}{8}$ in simplest form, divide the numerator and denominator by 2.

$$\frac{6}{8} = \frac{6 \div 2}{8 \div 2} = \frac{3}{4}$$

$$1\frac{6}{8} = 1\frac{3}{4}$$

Number Sense and Operations

Compare and Order Numbers

You can use a number line to compare two numbers. Use this number line to place several numbers in order by value.

> **Remember**
> < means *less than*
> > means *greater than*

On the number line, 2 comes before 5, so 2 *is less than* 5, or $2 < 5$. 8 comes after 6, so 8 *is greater than* 6, or $8 > 6$. Also, 6 is greater than 5, so all of these numbers could be written in order as $2 < 5 < 6 < 8$.

You can also use place value to compare and order numbers. To compare two numbers that have a *different* number of digits, the number with fewer digits is less. For example, $6 < 67$, $45 < 455$, and $32 < 329$.

To compare two numbers with the *same* number of digits, begin by lining them up by place value. Begin at the left and find the first place where the digits are different. For example, compare 346 and 359. Look at the digits in the hundreds place. Both numbers have a 3 in the hundreds place. Look at the tens place. 346 has a 4 in the tens place, and 359 has a 5 in the tens place. Since $4 < 5$, $346 < 359$.

Compare two fractions that have the *same* denominator by comparing the numerators. $5 < 7$, so $\frac{5}{12} < \frac{7}{12}$. $5 > 3$, so $\frac{5}{8} > \frac{3}{8}$.

Example

Which number is the *greatest*: $\frac{2}{4}$, $\frac{3}{4}$, or $\frac{1}{4}$? ____________

Compare $\frac{2}{4}$, $\frac{3}{4}$, and $\frac{1}{4}$ by comparing their numerators.

Since $1 < 2 < 3$, $\frac{1}{4} < \frac{2}{4} < \frac{3}{4}$. $\frac{3}{4}$ has the greatest value.

Round Whole Numbers

When you *round* a number, you find another number that is close in value. For example, round 123 and 128 to the nearest ten.

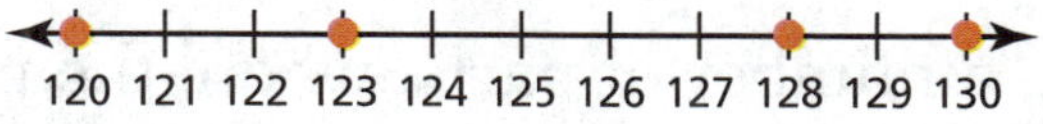

Look at the number line. You can see that 128 is closer to 130 than 120. You can also see that 123 is closer to 120 than 130.

Remember

Rounding a number makes it easier for you to estimate an answer. See page 38 for help on estimating.

When rounding numbers without the use of a number line, you have to use place value. For example, round 128 to the nearest ten. Look at the digit in the tens place, 2. Now, look at the digit in the place to its right, 8. When the number in the next place is *greater than or equal to 5*, add 1 to the place you are rounding to. Then change all digits to the right of it to zeros. 128 rounded to the tens place is 130.

128 → 8 is greater than 5
+1
130

Round 123 to the nearest ten. The digit in the ones place is less than 5. When the number in the next place *is less than 5*, the digit in the place you are rounding to stays the same. Change all digits to the right of it to zeros. 123 rounded to the tens place is 120.

123 → 3 is less than 5
120

Example

Round 1462 to the nearest hundred.

____

The digit in the place to the right of the hundreds place is 6. Since 6 is greater than or equal to 5, add 1 to the 4 in the hundreds place. Change all digits to the right of the hundreds place to zeros.

Add Fractions

Like fractions have denominators that are the same. The fractions $\frac{1}{5}$ and $\frac{2}{5}$ are like fractions. Each fraction represents a number of parts, where the parts are equal in size. 1 *fifth* + 2 *fifths* = 3 *fifths*. To add two fractions with like denominators, add the numerators and keep the common denominator.

$$\frac{1}{5} + \frac{2}{5} = \frac{1+2}{5} = \frac{3}{5}$$

When the sum of the numerators of two fractions is greater than 1, write the answer as a mixed number.

$$\frac{3}{4} + \frac{3}{4} = \frac{6}{4} = 1\frac{1}{2}$$

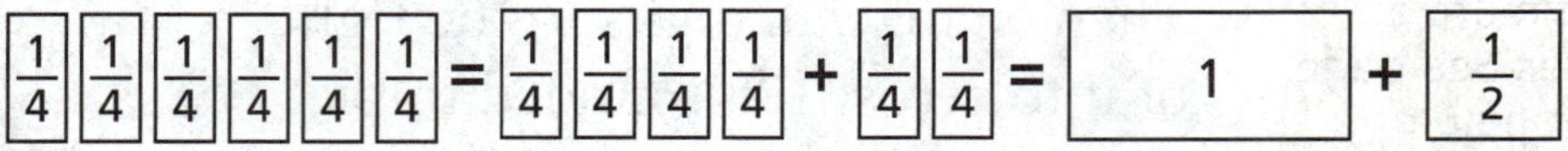

Remember

An improper fraction has a numerator greater than its denominator.

Simplify all improper fractions.

Example:

$\frac{12}{8} = 12 \div 8 = 1R4$

$= 1\frac{4}{8} = 1\frac{1}{2}$

To add two mixed fractions, add the whole parts and then the fraction parts.

$$1\frac{1}{7} + 2\frac{2}{7} = (1 + 2) + (\frac{1}{7} + \frac{2}{7}) = 3\frac{3}{7}$$

Example

$$\frac{6}{7} + \frac{2}{7} = \square$$

____

Add the numerators and keep the common denominator.

$\frac{6}{7} + \frac{2}{7} = \frac{6+2}{7} = \frac{8}{7}$. Write the improper fraction $\frac{8}{7}$ in simplest form. Since $8 \div 7 = 1R1$, then $\frac{8}{7} = \frac{7}{7} + \frac{1}{7} = 1\frac{1}{7}$.

Subtract Fractions

To subtract two fractions with the same denominator, subtract the numerators and keep the common denominator.

$$\frac{7}{8} - \frac{3}{8} = \frac{7-3}{8} = \frac{4}{8}$$

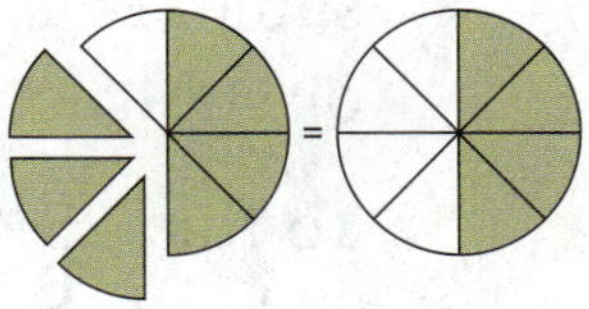

Write the answer in simplest form. To simplify the answer, find a number that divides evenly into both 4 and 8.

$$\frac{4}{8} = \frac{4 \div 4}{8 \div 4} = \frac{1}{2}$$

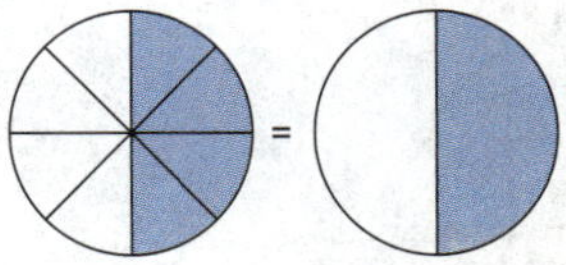

Remember

Dividing a fraction by 1 does not change its value. A number divided by itself equals 1.
Examples:

$\frac{4}{4} = \frac{1}{1} = 1$

$\frac{12}{12} = \frac{1}{1} = 1$

Example

$\frac{8}{9} - \frac{5}{9} = \square$

____

A bag contains $\frac{11}{12}$ cup of rice. Libby uses $\frac{5}{12}$ cup of the rice for dinner.

How much rice is left in the bag?

____

Subtract the numerators and keep the common denominator. Divide both the numerator and denominator by 3 to find the simplest form.

$$\frac{8}{9} - \frac{5}{9} = \frac{8-5}{9} = \frac{3}{9} = \frac{3 \div 3}{9 \div 3} = \frac{1}{3}$$

Follow the same steps for this problem.

$$\frac{11}{12} - \frac{5}{12} = \frac{6}{12} = \frac{6 \div 6}{12 \div 6} = \frac{1}{2}$$

Add and Subtract Decimal Numbers

Adding and subtracting decimals is a lot like adding and subtracting whole numbers. The idea of regrouping is the same. Place values must be aligned. In addition, when adding or subtracting decimals, decimal points must be aligned.

> **Remember**
> Zeros may be added to the end of any decimal number without changing its value.
> 5.6 = 5.60 = 5.600

To find 23.4 − 8.92, line up the decimal points. Add a zero to the right of the 4 to act as a place holder: 23.4 = 23.40. The problem will look like this:

$$\begin{array}{r} 12\ \ 13 \\ 1\ \ 2\ \ \ 3\ 10 \\ \not{2}\ \not{3}.\not{4}\ \not{0} \\ -\ 8.9\ 2 \\ \hline 1\ 4.4\ 8 \end{array}$$

Once the decimal points are lined up, subtract as usual. Then bring the decimal point straight down to the answer.

Example

12.7 − 4.56 = ☐

____

$$\begin{array}{r} 6\,10 \\ 12.\not{7}\,\not{0} \\ -\ 4.5\,6 \\ \hline 8.1\,4 \end{array}$$

For both problems line up the decimal points. Add a zero as a place holder. Subtract and bring the decimal point down to the answer.

Carl finished the race in 13.8 minutes. Marty finished in 15.2 minutes. How much faster was Carl's time?

____

$$\begin{array}{rl} 4\ 12 & \\ 1\not{5}.\not{2} & \text{Marty's time} \\ -\ 13.8 & \text{Carl's time} \\ \hline 1.4 & \text{minutes} \end{array}$$

Write Number Sentences

A *number sentence* is a mathematical sentence that contains an equal sign. You can use a number sentence to model a problem.

When you write a number sentence, use numbers, operations, and an equal sign to represent the words and numbers in the problem. This chart shows basic operations and the common words that are used to describe them.

Common English Words for Basic Operations

+	−	×	÷	=
increase	decrease	of	each	equals
add	subtract	multiply	quotient	is
more	less	product	fraction	are

Write the following word sentence as a number sentence.

"Two more than twice three is eight."

Two more than is "2 +."
Twice three is "2 × 3."
Is is "=." The number sentence is $2 + (2 \times 3) = 8$.

Example

Hillary read 20 books in 5 weeks. She read the same number of books each week. How many books did she read each week?

What number sentence describes the number of books Hillary read each week?

____

Look for key words that describe a mathematical operation. The phrase "each week," suggests division. The problem says the "same number of books each week." The number of books is the dividend and the number of weeks is the divisor.

Estimation

> **Remember**
> When rounding remember these 2 quick rules: *greater than or equal to 5*, round up *less than 5*, the number stays the same.

An *estimate* is a number that is close to another number in value. An estimate is useful for checking the answer to a problem. An estimate usually involves rounding the numbers in the problem so the problem is easier to solve.

Morten drives 6.78 miles to work each day. He finds a shortcut that makes his drive 3.31 miles shorter. Estimate the distance Morten drives to work using the shortcut.

The distance Morten drives to work using the shortcut is the difference between the original distance (6.78 miles) and the distance he saves using the shortcut (3.31 miles). To estimate this difference, round to the nearest whole number and subtract. 6.78 miles rounds to 7 miles. 3.31 miles rounds to 3 miles. 7 − 3 = 4.

Morten drives about 4 miles to work using the shortcut.

Example

Estimate to the nearest hundred.

428 + 282 is about ☐.

____

Alex bought a gift that cost $5.68, including tax. He paid $2.09 to have the gift wrapped. About how much did Alex pay in all?

____

428 rounds to 400. 282 rounds to 300. 400 + 300 = 700.

$5.68 rounded to the nearest whole dollar is $6.00.
$2.09 rounded to the nearest whole dollar is $2.00.
Add the rounded amounts. $6.00 + $2.00 = $8.00.

Problem Solving

Often a problem can be solved in more than one way. When solving a problem, always read it carefully. Be sure you understand the information in the problem and the question it asks. Then decide how to solve the problem. As you work, organize the information in the problem.

Nathan's mother is 32 years old. Nathan is 6 years younger than half his mother's age. How old is Nathan?

Read the problem. Organize the information. Then decide how to solve the problem.

For this problem you can write a number sentence using the information given. Nathan's age is 6 years younger than half of his mother's age. Let n represent what you need to find, Nathan's age. "Half his mother's age" is $32 \div 2$. "6 years younger" is $-\ 6$ The number sentence is $n = 32 \div 2 - 6$.

Solve the number sentence. $n = 32 \div 2 - 6$
$n = 16 - 6 = 10$

Nathan is 10 years old.

Remember to check your answer to make sure it is reasonable.

HINT

There are other ways to solve a problem:

- Find a Pattern
- Relate to Another Problem
- Break a Problem into Smaller Parts
- Guess and Check
- Work Backwards

Example

Sylvia picked up some leaves in the park. She gave 5 away to her friend. Then she picked up 8 more leaves. Sylvia took 18 leaves home. How many leaves did she first pick up?

____

Let x represent the number of leaves Sylvia first picked up.
$18 = 8 - 5 + x$.
$18 = 3 + x$ What number added to 3 is equal to 18?
$18 = 3 + 15$ Sylvia must have first picked up 15 leaves.

Number Sense and Operations

1

Vicki drove through a tunnel that was 29,530 meters long. Which digit in the number 29,530 is in the hundreds place?

A 2

B 3

C 5

D 9

2

One mile is equivalent to 5280 feet. Which digit in the number 5280 is in the tens place?

A 8

B 5

C 2

D 0

3

Deanne bought a car for $13,468. What is 13,468 rounded to the nearest hundred?

A 10,000

B 13,400

C 13,470

D 13,500

4

This chart shows the names and heights of the five tallest mountains in Colorado.

Mountain Name	Height (in feet)
Blanca Peak	14,345
La Plata Peak	14,361
Mt. Elbert	14,433
Mt. Harvard	14,420
Mt. Massive	14,421

Which height is the *greatest*?

A 14,345 feet

B 14,433 feet

C 14,361 feet

D 14,421 feet

5

A roll of stickers was divided among 5 friends. Natalie got $\frac{2}{12}$ of the stickers, Pedro got $\frac{4}{12}$, Nelda got $\frac{3}{12}$, Jim got $\frac{1}{12}$, and Emily got $\frac{2}{12}$.

Who got the *least* number of stickers?

A Emily
B Jim
C Nelda
D Pedro

6

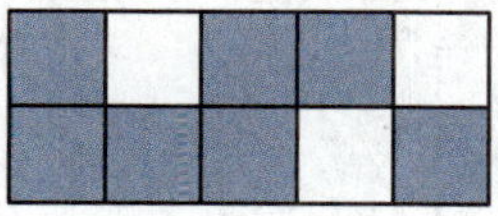

What fraction of the rectangle is shaded?

A	**B**	**C**	**D**
$\frac{3}{4}$	$\frac{7}{10}$	$\frac{1}{2}$	$\frac{3}{10}$

7

$\frac{3}{5}$ of the socks in Terry's drawer are white. $\frac{1}{5}$ of the socks in his drawer are blue. What fraction of Terry's socks are either white or blue?

A	**B**	**C**	**D**
$\frac{4}{5}$	$\frac{3}{5}$	$\frac{1}{2}$	$\frac{4}{10}$

8

Kara used $\frac{5}{8}$ roll of blue yarn and $\frac{7}{8}$ roll of orange yarn to make a scarf. How many rolls of yarn did she use in all?

A	**B**	**C**	**D**
$1\frac{1}{4}$	$1\frac{3}{8}$	$1\frac{1}{2}$	$1\frac{5}{8}$

9

Hiroko bought 1 gallon of stain to use on a new bookshelf. She used $\frac{1}{6}$ gallon of the stain. How many gallons of stain does she have left?

A	B	C	D
0	$\frac{1}{2}$	$\frac{2}{3}$	$\frac{5}{6}$

10

The mass of a penny is 2.5 grams. The mass of a dime is 2.268 grams. How much more mass does a penny have than a dime?

A 0.232 grams

B 0.342 grams

C 0.368 grams

D 0.768 grams

11

Greg weighs 51.2 pounds. One year ago he weighed 10.4 pounds less than he does now. How much did Greg weigh a year ago?

A 40.8 pounds

B 41.8 pounds

C 60.6 pounds

D 61.6 pounds

12

Nadia had 5 dolls. She gave 2 to her sister. What number sentence describes the number of dolls Nadia has left?

A $5 - \square = 2$

B $5 + \square = 2$

C $5 - 2 = \square$

D $5 + 2 = \square$

13

Wendell runs the same distance each day. He runs 14 miles each week. What number sentence describes the number of miles Wendell runs in one day?

A $7 + \square = 14$

B $14 \div \square = 7$

C $14 - 7 = \square$

D $14 \div 7 = \square$

14

The high school held a bake sale to raise money for new gym equipment. The chart shows how many muffins members from each class sold.

Grade	Number of Muffins Sold
10th	177
11th	106
12th	184

What is the best estimate for the number of muffins that were sold in all?

A 200

B 300

C 400

D 500

15

Ginny wants to buy a book that costs $7.13, but she only has $5.22. Which is the best estimate of how much more money Ginny needs to buy the book?

A $1.00

B $2.00

C $3.00

D $4.00

16

Isaiah had $12.50 when he left for the mall. He bought a large pretzel for $2.75 and he bought a hat. Isaiah had $3.25 left when he got home. How much did the hat cost?

A $5.50

B $5.75

C $6.00

D $6.50

Patterns, Relationships, and Algebra

Number Patterns

A *number pattern* is a list of numbers that follow a rule. The *rule* tells the relationship between the numbers in the pattern. The three dots at the end mean the pattern continues. Look at this example.

4, 8, 12, 16, 20, ...

The second number is 4 more than the first: 4 + 4 = 8. The third number is 4 more than the second: 8 + 4 = 12, and so on. Since the numbers increase by 4 each time, the rule is "add 4."

Sometimes the rule for a pattern uses two operations.

2, 5, 4, 7, 6, 9, ...

Here, the second number is 3 more than the first, but the third number is 1 less than the second. These two operations are repeated. This rule is "add 3, subtract 1."

To find the next number in a number pattern, look at the numbers that are next to each other. Find how these number are related. Write the rule that describes the relationship. Then use the rule to find the next number.

Remember

When the rule for a pattern uses addition or subtraction, the numbers have a *common difference*.

When the rule for a pattern uses multiplication or division, the numbers have a *common ratio*.

Example

What are the next two numbers in this pattern? ______

1, 3, 6, 8, 11, ___, ___, ...

Find the pattern. To get from 1 to 3, you can "add 2" or "multiply by 3." To get from 3 to 6, you can "add 3" or "multiply by 2." To get from 6 to 8, you "add 2"; and from 8 to 11, you "add 3." The rule is "add 2, add 3."

Use the rule to find the next two numbers.

11 + 2 = 13, and 13 + 3 = 16.

Geometric Patterns

Geometric patterns are a series of shapes that follow a rule. A rule for a geometric pattern describes how the shapes repeat.

To find the next shape in a geometric pattern, look at the pattern and identify the shapes. Notice how they change the order. Write a rule that describes the change. Use the rule to find the next shape in the pattern.

Remember

Geometric patterns may use color as well as shape to create a pattern.

Problems with geometric patterns may ask you to find the missing shape. Look at this pattern.

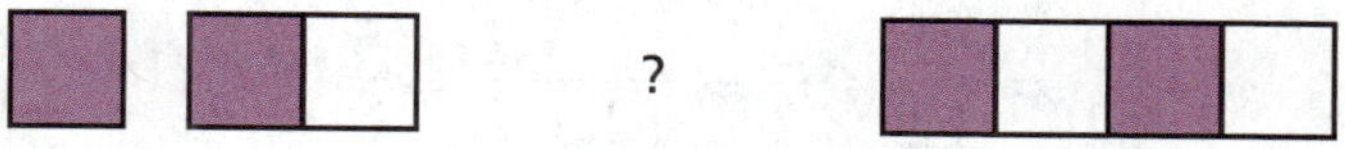

The first figure is a square. The second figure is two squares. The fourth figure is 4 squares. The missing figure must have three squares. It also must look something like the second and fourth shapes.

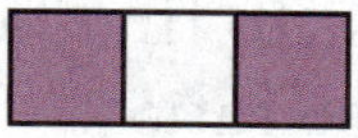

Example

What is the next shape in the pattern?__________________

The first three shapes in the pattern are: red triangle, green circle, blue square. The next two are a red triangle and a green circle. The next shape will likely be a blue square. The geometric pattern follows a rule for both color (red, green, blue) and shape (triangle, circle, square).

Ratios

A *ratio* shows a comparison of two numbers and is often written as a fraction. For example, in a class with 10 boys and 12 girls, the ratio of boys to girls is 10 to 12. The ratio of girls to all students in the class is 12 to 22. This chart shows three ways to write a ratio.

Comparison	Ratio in words	Ratio as a fraction	Ratio with a colon
a ratio of 10 boys to 12 girls.	10 to 12	$\frac{10}{12}$	10:12

A ratio in the form of a fraction may be simplified.

$$\frac{10}{12} = \frac{10}{12} \div \frac{2}{2} = \frac{10 \div 2}{12 \div 2} = \frac{5}{6}$$

There are 5 boys for every 6 girls in the class.

A car that travels 300 yards in 10 seconds travels at a ratio of $\frac{300 \text{ yards}}{10 \text{ seconds}}$. The ratio compares a number of yards to a number of seconds. To find how far the car can travel in one second, simplify the ratio.

$$\frac{300 \text{ yards}}{10 \text{ seconds}} = \frac{300 \div 10}{10 \div 10} = \frac{30}{1} = 30 \text{ yards per second}$$

The car travels 30 yards in 1 second.

Remember

To multiply fractions, multiply the numerators and multiply the denominators.

Example:

$\frac{2}{3} \times \frac{1}{5} = \frac{2}{15}$

Example

A delivery driver delivers packages to 25 homes in 4 hours.

How many homes can she deliver packages to in 8 hours?

____

The delivery driver delivers packages at a ratio of 25 homes per 4 hours, or $\frac{25 \text{ homes}}{4 \text{ hrs}}$. Multiply this fraction by 8 hours.

$$\frac{25 \text{ homes}}{4 \not{\text{hours}}} \times 8 \not{\text{hours}} = \frac{25}{4} \times \frac{8}{1} = \frac{200}{4} = 50 \text{ homes}$$

Number Sentences

A *number sentence* is an equation that uses numbers and math symbols, including an equal sign (=). It may use a box in place of a number. Use the information in the number sentence to find the number that goes in the box.

$$9 + \square = 15$$

Think of the number sentence in words: "9 plus *some number* equals 15." To find the answer, think of the number you would add to 9 to get 15. The answer is 6. Check your answer by reading the number sentence again. "9 plus 6 equals 15."

Remember

Addition and Subtraction are opposite operations.

Multiplication and Division are opposite operations.

Look at these number sentences:

$$32 + \square = 40 \qquad 40 - 32 = \square$$

The solution to both problems is 8. Notice how the problems are related. The number you add to 32 to get 40 is the same number you get when you subtract 32 from 40.

Look at these number sentences: $5 \times \square = 15 \quad 15 \div \square = 5$

The solution to both problems is 3. Again, notice how the two problems are related.

Example

Find the solution to each number sentence.

$r + 5 = 6$ ______	$6 - 5 = r$ ______
$10 \times \square = 100$ ______	$100 \div \square = 10$ ______

The solution to the addition and subtraction problems is $r = 1$, because $1 + 5 = 6$ and $6 - 5 = 1$. The solution to the multiplication and division problems is 10, because $10 \times 10 = 100$ and $100 \div 10 = 10$.

![Skill REVIEW]

Patterns, Relationships, and Algebra

1

What is the next number in the pattern?

1, 5, 9, 13, 17, ...

A 19 **C** 21
B 20 **D** 22

2

What is the next number in the pattern?

3, 6, 12, 24, 48, ...

A 96 **C** 60
B 72 **D** 54

3

What is the missing number in the pattern?

126, 105, 84, ___, 42, 21

A 83 **C** 63
B 73 **D** 53

4

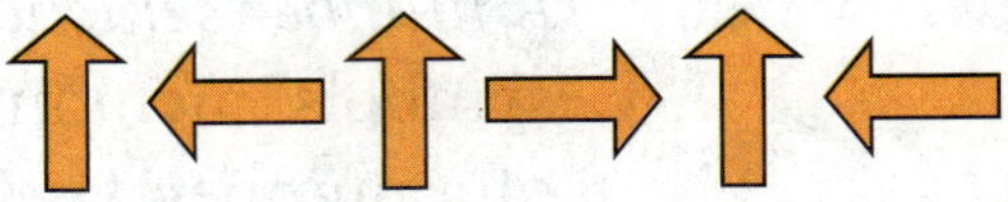

What is the next shape in the pattern?

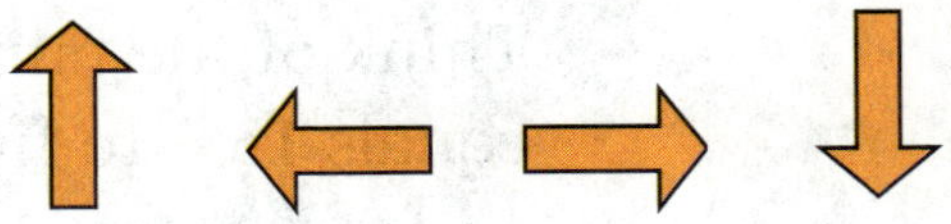

A **B** **C** **D**

5

What is the next shape in the pattern?

A **B** **C** **D**

6

What number makes this number sentence true?

$$11 + \square = 19$$

A 7 **C** 20
B 8 **D** 30

7

What number makes this number sentence true?

$$4 \times \square = 16$$

A 4 **C** 20
B 12 **D** 64

8

What is the value of *a*?

$$12 \times 2 = a$$

A 6 **C** 22
B 14 **D** 24

9

If $s + 8 = 16$, which of these statements must be true?

A $s = 16 + 8$ **C** $s = 16 \times 8$
B $s = 16 - 8$ **D** $s = 16 \div 8$

10

A bag of marbles contains 3 red marbles, 4 blue marbles, and 6 yellow marbles. What is the ratio of red marbles to all marbles?

A $\frac{3}{4}$ **B** $\frac{6}{13}$ **C** $\frac{4}{9}$ **D** $\frac{3}{13}$

11

A pencil case has 3 pens and 5 pencils in it. Which of the following does *not* show the ratio of pens to pencils?

A 3.5 **B** $\frac{3}{5}$ **C** 3:5 **D** 3 to 5

12

Zula checked her pulse. She found that her heart beat 12 times in ten seconds. At this rate, how many times would Zula's heart beat in one minute? (Hint: 1 minute = 60 seconds)

A 72 **C** 108
B 90 **D** 120

Skill FOCUS

Data, Statistics, and Probability

Interpret Data: Charts and Pictographs

This chart shows the five tallest buildings in the United States. It gives each building's name and height. Which is the tallest?

> **HINT**
> The title of a chart or pictograph tells what information is in the chart or pictograph.

Look in the column labeled *Height*. The largest value is 1450 feet next to the name *Sears Tower*. The Sears Tower is the tallest building in the United States.

Five Tallest Buildings

Building	Height (in feet)
Aon Centre, Chicago	1100
Chrysler Building, New York	1000
Empire State Building, New York	1250
John Hancock Center, Chicago	1100
Sears Tower, Chicago	1450

This pictograph shows the heights of the highest waterfalls in the United States. It uses symbols for the waterfall heights. For example, the pictograph shows that Ribbon Falls is 1,600 feet high.

Five Highest Waterfalls

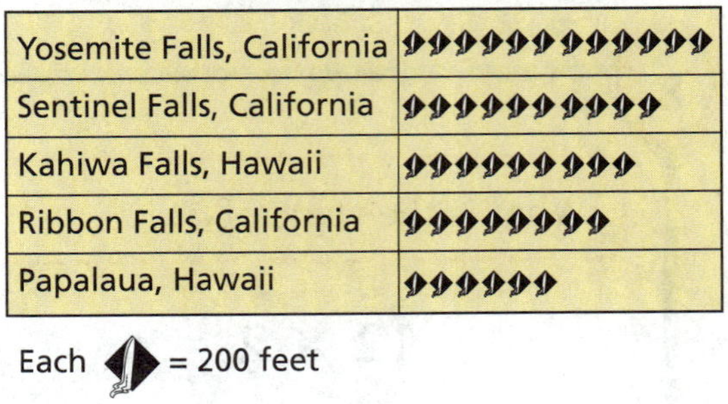

> **Remember**
> A key at the bottom of the pictograph tells what each symbol is for.

Example

This pictograph shows the most popular types of books for fourth graders in the school.

How many more students chose mystery books than adventure books?

____

Most Popular Books

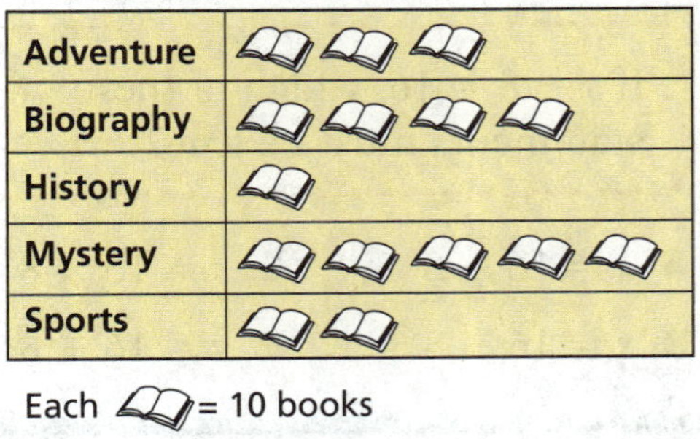

Subtract the number of symbols next to *Adventure* from the number of symbols next to *Mystery*: 5 − 3 = 2. Each book symbol represents 10 books. 20 more mystery books than adventure books were chosen.

Interpret Data: Bar Graphs and Circle Graphs

Bar graphs show values side by side. *Circle graphs* show parts of a whole. Both graphs compare data.

Remember

Use the scale on a bar graph to find the value of the bars.

When making a bar graph, remember to give it a title, label the side and the bottom, and the scale of the graph.

The Mills Elementary School choir planned a pizza party. Each student voted on the day of the week for the party. This bar graph has one bar for each day of the school week. The scale shows how many votes each day got.

A circle graph is a circle divided into pie-shaped pieces. Each piece stands for part of a set of data. This circle graph shows the same data as the bar graph above.

Wednesday and Thursday each got the same number of votes. These sections of the circle graph are equal.

Example

Linda asked one hundred people to name their favorite color. The graph below shows their answers.

How many more people named purple than orange as their favorite color?

____

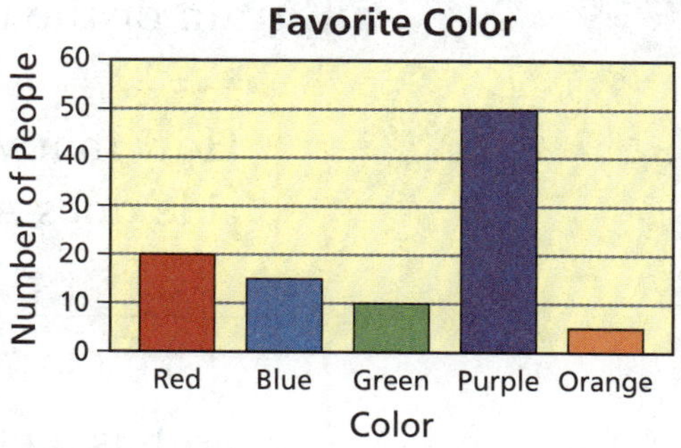

The bar for purple reaches 50, so 50 people picked purple.
The bar for orange reaches 5. Subtract: 50 − 5 = 45.

Combinations

A *combination* is a set of items in which the order of the items is not important. A *tree diagram* shows all the possible combinations that can be made with two or more sets of items.

Lana's dad is making her a birthday cake. She can have either chocolate or white cake, and either chocolate, strawberry, or vanilla icing. This tree diagram shows all the combinations of cake and icing that Lana can choose.

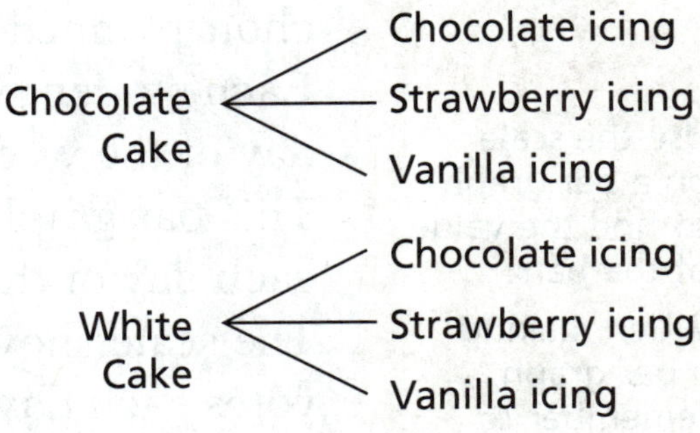

Lana can choose from 2 kinds of cake. For *each* kind of cake, she can have one of 3 three flavors of icing. $2 \times 3 = 6$. So, there are 6 different possible combinations of cake and icing.

If Lana tells her father she wants strawberry cake with chocolate icing, she has made an *impossible combination*. Strawberry is not in the set of cake flavors she has to choose from.

Remember

Multiply the number of choices for each set of items to get the number of possible combinations.

Example

At the end of a day at the zoo, Alan has time to see one more animal and go on one more ride. He can see either the elephants, monkeys, tigers, or zebras, and ride either the train or the merry-go-round.

How many possible combinations of one animal and one ride does Alan have to choose from?

____

Alan has a choice of 4 animals and 2 rides. He has $4 \times 2 = 8$ possible combinations to choose from.

> **Remember**
> No outcome is certain unless it is the only possible outcome. No outcome is impossible unless it is not a possible outcome.
> An outcome that is unlikely is one that probably won't happen, but is not impossible.

Probability of a Simple Event

Probability is a way to describe how likely it is for something to happen. All choices are possible *outcomes*, or results, of an experiment. An event is an outcome that really happens.

An event that will probably happen is *likely*, but is not certain. An event that is *unlikely* is one that probably won't happen, but is not impossible. Look at the spinner below.

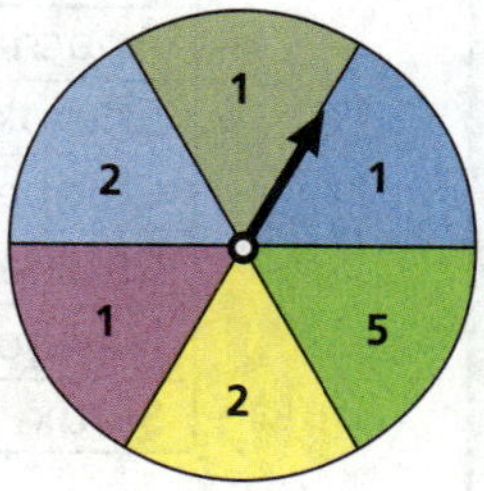

Look at the spinner on the right. Is it likely that the pointer will stop on 5? What is the most likely outcome of a single spin? The spinner has 6 equal sections, so it is *equally likely* that the pointer will stop on any one section. Only one section has the number 5. So, it is possible for the pointer to stop on the number five. However, this is an unlikely event. It is more likely that the pointer will stop on 1 or 2.

There are more 1's than any other number on the spinner, so the pointer is *most* likely to stop on a 1. There are other numbers on the spinner, so it is not certain that the pointer will stop on a 1.

Example

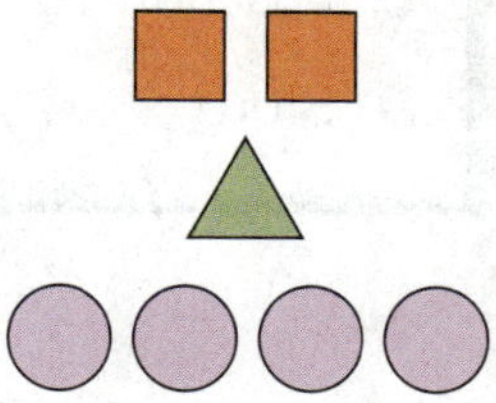

Jenny is given this set of shapes. She chooses one shape without looking. Is it likely that Jenny will pick a circle?

There are 4 circles and 7 shapes in all. More than half of the shapes are circles. So, it is likely that Jenny will pick a circle.

Skill REVIEW

Data, Statistics, and Probability

1

This chart shows the number of people in several American Indian tribes in the year 2000.

Number of People in Native American Tribes, in 2000

Tribe	Population
Apache	50,051
Cherokee	308,132
Chippewa	105,907
Choctaw	87,349
Navajo	219,198
Sioux	103,255

Which tribe had between 80,000 and 100,000 people in the year 2000?

A Apache

B Choctaw

C Navajo

D Sioux

2

The Shah bakery has 4 salespeople. The pictograph shows how many pies each sold on Monday.

Pies Sold at the Shah Bakery

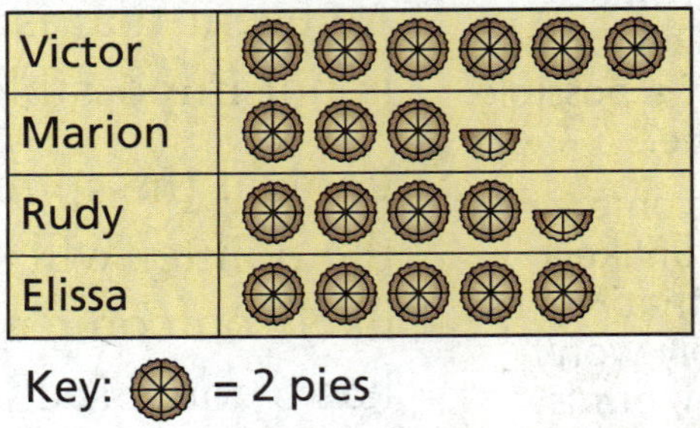

How many pies did Marion and Elissa sell all together?

A	**B**	**C**	**D**
17	16	$8\frac{1}{2}$	$3\frac{1}{2}$

3

Ricky looked up how fast some animals can move. He used the data to make this bar graph.

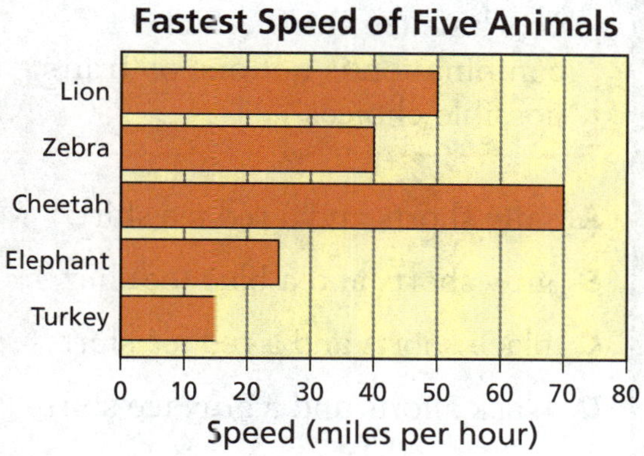

Which animal can move exactly twice as fast as an elephant?

A Cheetah

B Lion

C Turkey

D Zebra

4

Students at Marnie's school went to different kinds of camps last summer. This circle graph shows the camps that students went to. Each student went to only one kind of camp.

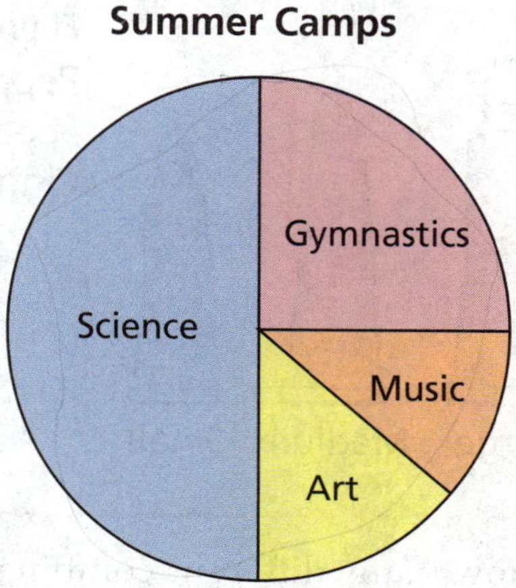

Which camp did the greatest number of students go to last summer?

A Art

B Gymnastics

C Music

D Science

5

Henrik needs to buy a new tube of toothpaste. He can get peppermint, spearmint, or cinnamon flavor. Each flavor comes in large, medium, and small sizes.

Flavors
Peppermint
Spearmint
Cinnamon

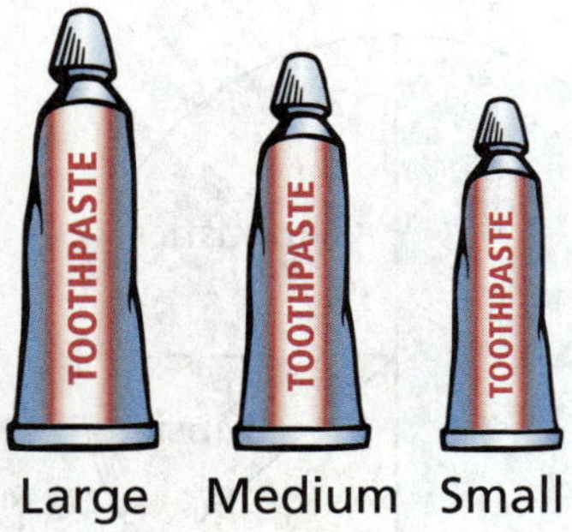

How many different combinations of size and flavor of toothpaste does Henrik have to choose from?

A 3

B 6

C 9

D 12

6

For her gym uniform, Tran can choose between gray shorts and black shorts, and a red tee shirt or a blue tee shirt. Which combination is not one of Tran's possible choices?

A gray shorts and a red tee shirt

B gray shorts and a blue tee shirt

C black shorts and a red tee shirt

D black shorts and a gray tee shirt

7

Mr. Walker put 3 green counters and 10 purple counters into a hat. If he pulls a counter without looking, what is the probability that he will pull a green one?

A certain

B likely

C unlikely

D impossible

8

Gita picked a card from this set of cards without looking.

What card is Gita *least likely* to pick?

A **B** **C** **D**

Skill FOCUS

Geometry and Measurement

Solid Figures

HINT

Figures such as triangles, squares, and circles are plane figures.

A *solid figure* has length, width, and height. Figures such as prisms and cylinders are solid figures. The *faces*, or surfaces, of a solid figure are *plane figures*, or flat shapes. For example, a cube has six square faces.

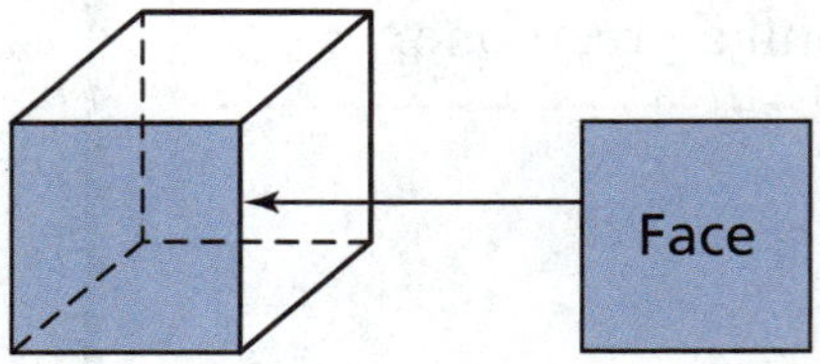

An *edge* of a solid figure is a line segment where two faces meet. A *vertex* is a point where three or more edges meet.

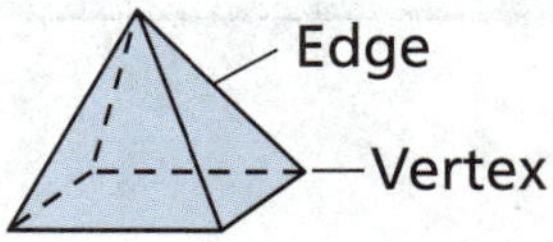

Remember

A sphere has no faces, edges, or vertices.

Here are some common solid figures.

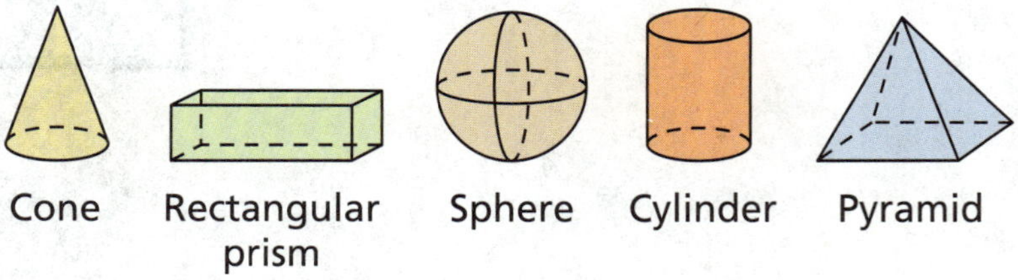

Example

Which solids above have at least one face that is a circle?

____

The flat surfaces of a solid are its faces. Look at the surfaces of each solid. The base of the cone is a circle. The cylinder has 2 faces that are circles. The sphere has no flat surfaces, so it has no faces.

Parallel and Perpendicular Lines

> **HINT**
> Where two lines *intersect*, they cross a point.

Two lines that never intersect and are always the same distance apart are *parallel*.

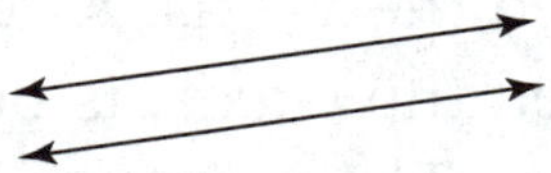

Parallel Lines

An angle that forms a square corner is a *right angle*. When two lines that intersect form right angles, the lines are *perpendicular*.

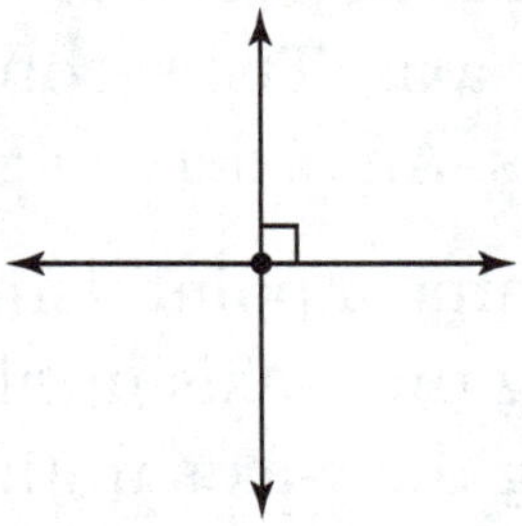

Perpendicular Lines

Example

Look at square *ABCD*. Name a pair of segments in the square that are parallel. Name a pair of segments that are perpendicular.

____

____

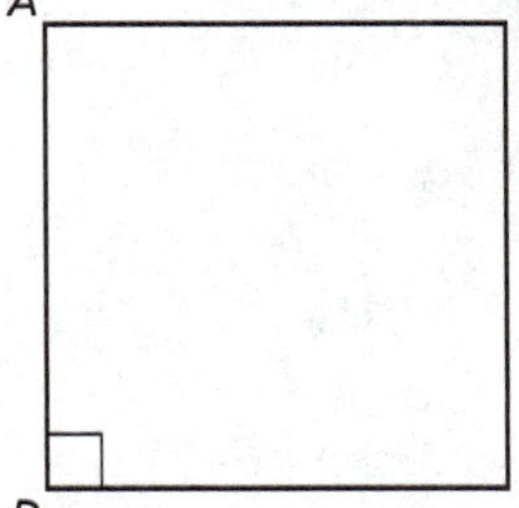

The sides of a square are two sets of parallel line segments. The two pairs of parallel segments in this square are $\overline{AB}$ and $\overline{DC}$, and $\overline{AD}$ and $\overline{BC}$. There are four pairs of perpendicular line segments in this square: $\overline{AD}$ is perpendicular to $\overline{AB}$ and $\overline{DC}$. $\overline{BC}$ is perpendicular to $\overline{BA}$ and $\overline{CD}$.

Coordinate Plane

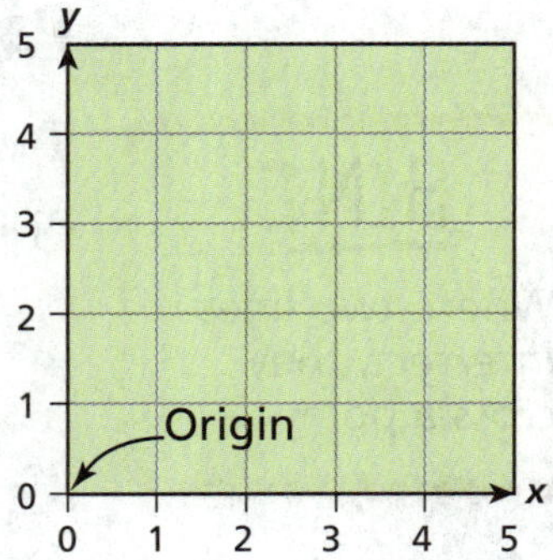

A *coordinate plane* is a special kind of grid. It is made up of a horizontal number line, called the *x*-axis. A vertical number line, called the *y*-axis, is perpendicular to the *x*-axis. The two axes intersect at a point called the *origin*.

Remember

An ordered pair tells where a point is in relationship to the *x*- and the *y*- axes.

You can name any point on a coordinate plane using an *ordered pair* of numbers. The first number names where a point is along the *x*-axis. The second number names where a point is along the *y*-axis. An ordered pair is also called the *x*- and *y*-coordinates.

To name a point using an ordered pair, start at the origin. Count along the *x*-axis until you reach the *x*-coordinate. Then count along the *y*-axis until you reach the *y*-coordinate.

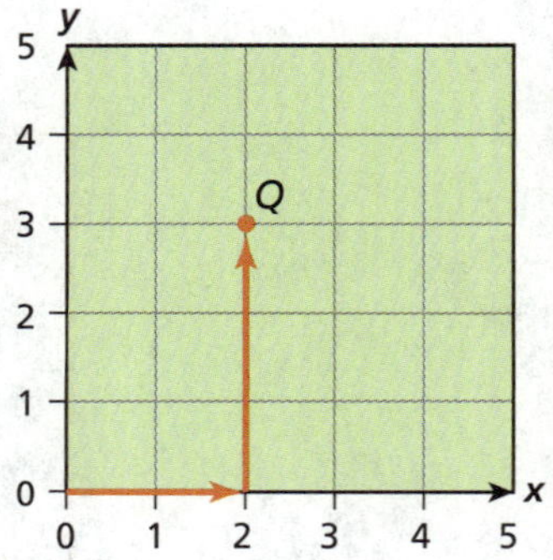

For example, to plot the point with coordinates (2, 3), start at the origin and move right 2 units. Then, move up 3 units. The coordinate plane contains point *Q* with coordinates (2, 3).

Example

Which point is located at (4, 3)?

____

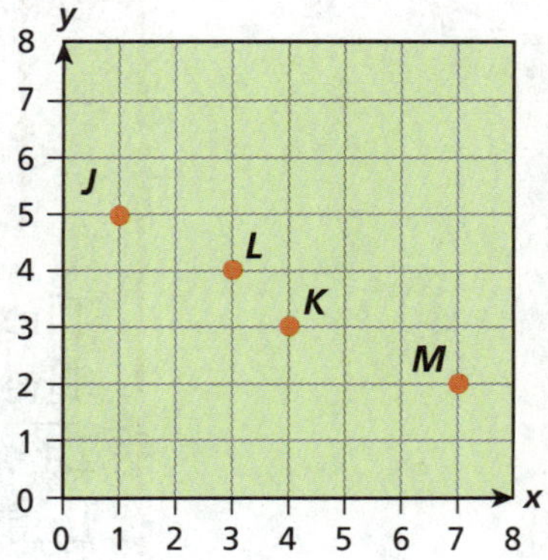

To find the point whose ordered pair is (4, 3), start at the origin. Then, move 4 spaces right and 3 spaces up.

Perimeter and Area

Every plane figure has a perimeter and an area. The *perimeter* is the distance around the figure. The *area* is a measure of the space inside the figure.

To find the perimeter of a shape, add the lengths of each of the sides. The figure shown has 5 sides with lengths 2, 5, 3, 6, and 3 inches. Its perimeter is:

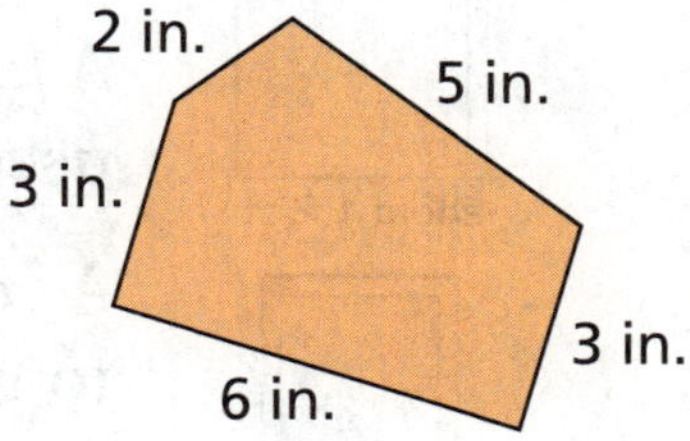

2 in. + 5 in. + 3 in. + 6 in. + 3 in. = 19 in.

Remember

A rectangle has two pairs of equal-length sides, so its perimeter is twice the length plus twice the width.

A square has four sides of equal length, so its perimeter is four times the length of one side.

The area of a figure is measured in square units. The rectangle shown is divided into 8 one-inch squares.

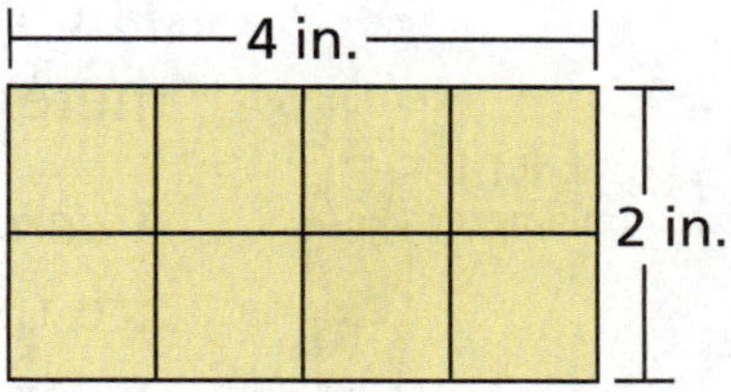

Since there are 8 one-inch squares inside the rectangle, the area of the rectangle is 8 square inches.

If a figure is measured in centimeters, the square units inside the figure would be measured in square centimeters.

Example

What is the perimeter of this figure?

____

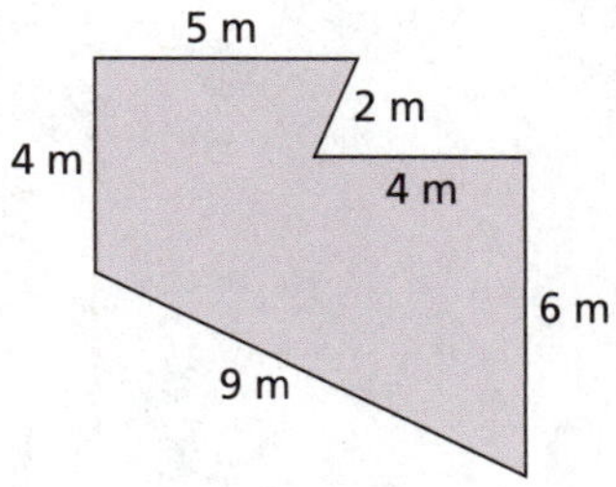

The perimeter is the distance around the figure. Add the lengths of all the sides:
4 m + 5 m + 2 m + 4 m + 6 m + 9 m = 30 m

Geometry and Measurement

Units of Measure

about 1 inch

about 1 foot

about 1 yard

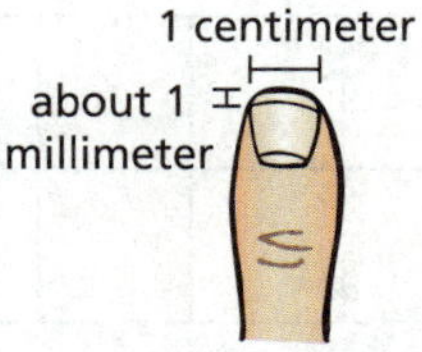

about 2 meters

The *customary units* of length are inches, feet, yards, and miles.

An *inch* is about the length of a paper clip. Inches are used to measure small lengths, such as the height of a drinking glass.

A *foot* is about the length of a sheet of notebook paper. Feet are used to measure larger lengths, such as the length of a desk.

A *yard* is 3 feet long, or about the width of a door. Yards are used to measure distances, such as the length of a soccer field.

A *mile* is used to measure very long distances, such as the distance between two cities.

The most common *metric units* of length are centimeters, meters, and kilometers.

A *centimeter* is about the length of your thumbnail. Centimeters are used to measure short objects, such as the length of a pencil. A centimeter can be divided into a smaller unit, called a *millimeter*. 1 cm = 10 mm.

A *meter* is about the same length as a yard. You could use meters to measure the length of a car.

A *kilometer* is a little more than three fifths of a mile. Like miles, kilometers are used to measure long distances, such as the length of a river.

Example

What units could you use to measure the width of a piano?

____

Centimeters or inches are too small. Kilometers or miles are too large. The best units to use are feet, yards, or meters.

Temperature

Remember
The symbol ° means "degrees." So °F is read as "degrees Fahrenheit" and °C is read as "degrees Celsius."

A *thermometer* is an instrument used to measure temperature. Temperature is usually measured in degrees Fahrenheit or degrees Celsius.

Some important temperatures in degrees Fahrenheit are:

32 °F – the temperature at which water freezes

70 °F – room temperature

212 °F – the temperature at which water boils

Some important temperatures in degrees Celsius are:

0 °C – the temperature at which water freezes

21 °C – room temperature

100 °C – the temperature at which water boils

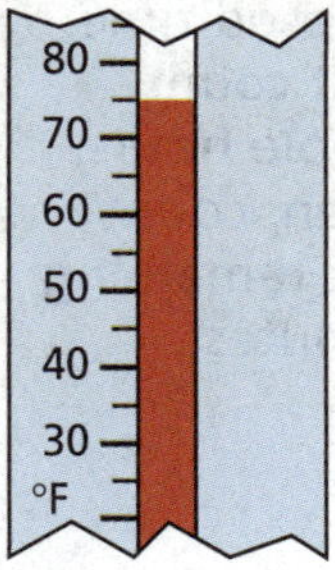

To read the thermometer shown, look at the number on the scale closest to the top of the red line. The red line reaches to the mark that is halfway between 70 and 80 degrees. So, the temperature is about 75 °F.

Example

What temperature is shown on the thermometer?

____

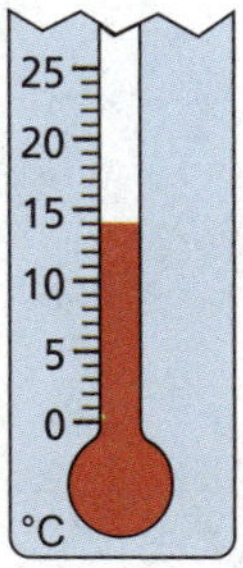

Find the number on the scale that is closest to the top of the red line. The red line reaches the fourth mark above 10. Each mark represents 1 °C. 10 + 4 = 14.

Elapsed Time

The time between two events is called *elapsed time*. For example:

Tanya runs from 3:30 to 5:20. How long did she run?

First count the whole hours. The elapsed time from 3:30 to 4:30 is 1 hour. Then count the remaining minutes. The elapsed time from 4:30 to 5:00 is 30 minutes. The elapsed time from 5:00 to 5:20 is another 20 minutes. The total elapsed time is:
1 hour + 30 minutes + 20 minutes = 1 hour 50 minutes.

HINT

The short hand on a clock gives the hours. The long hand gives the minutes.

Remember

When finding elapsed time, first count whole hours. Then, count the remaining minutes.

Example

Rand's softball game started at 5:45. It ended at 7:20. How long was the game?

____

The elapsed time from 5:45 to 6:45 is 1 hour. The elapsed time from 6:45 to 7:00 is 15 minutes. The elapsed time from 7:00 to 7:20 is another 20 minutes. The total elapsed time is 1 hour + 15 minutes + 20 minutes = 1 hour 35 minutes.

Cara's dance rehearsal lasts for about 2 hours and 45 minutes. Today rehearsal was over at 5:20. About what time did it start?

____

First find the time 2 hours before 5:20. 5:20 – 2 hours = 3:20. Then find the time 45 minutes before 3:20. Twenty minutes before 3:20 is 3:00. 45 minutes – 20 minutes = 25 minutes. Twenty-five minutes before 3:00 is 2:35.

Money

Money comes in the form of bills and coins. Different values are called *denominations*. Money is written in decimal form.

What is the total value of these bills and coins? Start with the money with the greatest value. The total value equals:

Remember

$0.01 = 1 penny
$0.05 = 1 nickel
$0.10 = 1 dime
$0.25 = 1 quarter
$1.00 = 1 dollar
$5.00 = 5 dollars

(1 × $5.00) + (1 × $1.00) +
(3 × $0.25)+ (1 × $0.10) +
(2 × $0.05) + (3 × $0.01) =
$5.00 + $1.00 + $0.75 + $0.10 + $0.10 + $0.03 = $6.98.

How much change should you get if you buy an item for $4.51 and pay for it with a 10-dollar bill?

$$\begin{array}{r} \$10.00 \\ -\ \$4.51 \\ \hline \$5.49 \end{array}$$

Example

The chart shows some ice cream prices.

What is the most expensive ice cream treat you can buy with the following money?

____

Item	Cost
1 scoop	$1.75
2 scoops	$2.25
3 scoops	$2.75
Banana Split	$3.50

Find the total value of the money.
(2 × $1.00) + (3 × 10¢) + (1 × 5¢) + (4 × 1¢) =
$2.00 + 30¢ + 5¢ + 4¢ = $2.00 + 39¢ = $2.39

Compare this amount to the prices. $2.25 < $2.39 < $2.75.
There is enough money for 2 scoops of ice cream.

Skill REVIEW

Geometry and Measurement

1

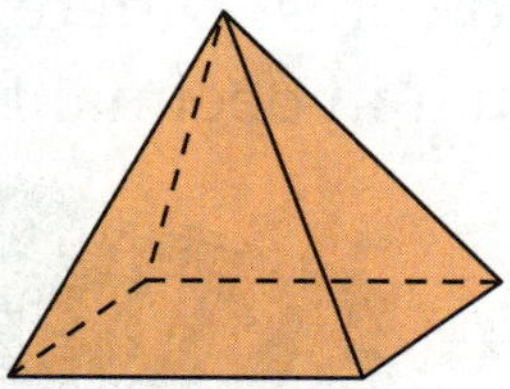

Which picture represents a top view of this solid?

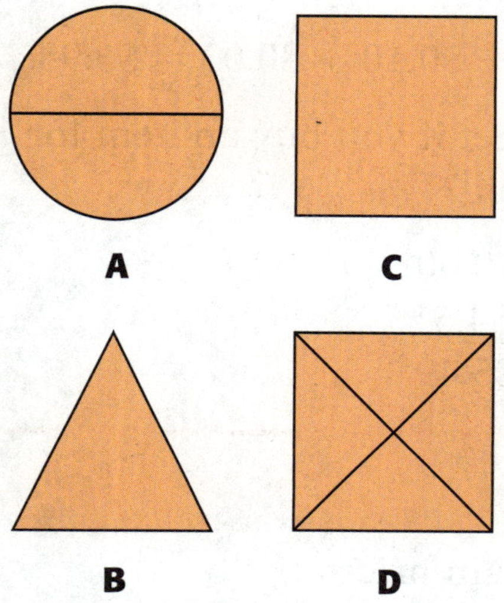

2

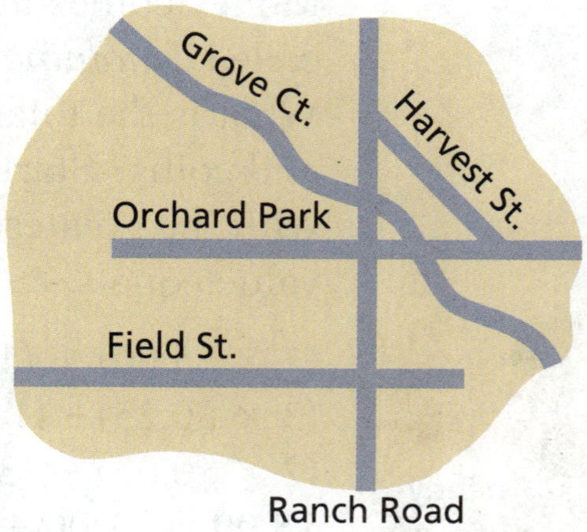

Which road is parallel to Orchard Park?

A Ranch Road

B Field Street

C Grove Court

D Harvest Street

3

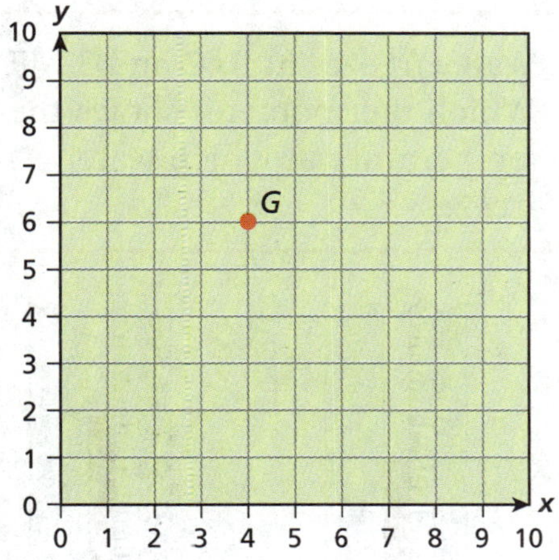

What is the ordered pair for point *G*?

A (4, 6)

B (6, 4)

C (3, 7)

D (7, 3)

4

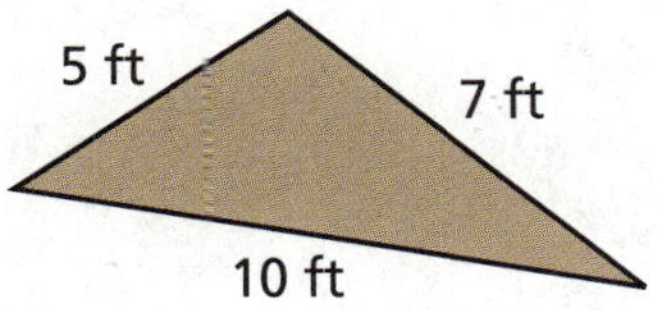

What is the perimeter of this triangle?

A 12 feet

B 22 feet

C 12 square feet

D 22 square feet

5

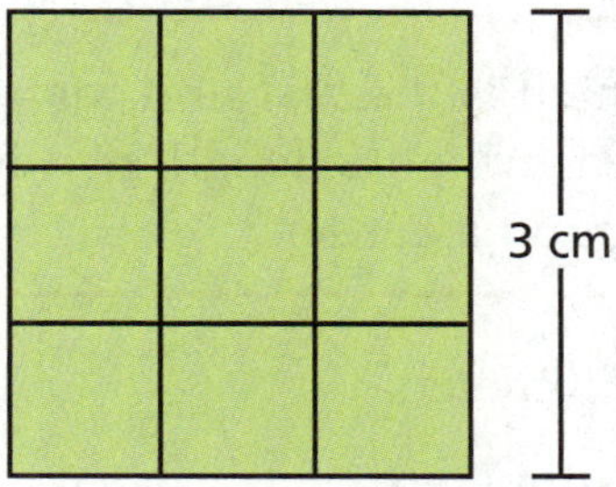

What is the area of this square?

A 9 centimeters

B 9 square centimeters

C 12 centimeters

D 12 square centimeters

6

Which measure could be the length of a calculator?

A 5 inches

B 5 feet

C 5 yards

D 5 miles

7

Which is the *best* unit for measuring the length of a fence around a garden?

A millimeters

B centimeters

C meters

D kilometers

8

Edgar went to lunch at 11:45 A.M. He got back to his desk at 1:10 P.M. How long was Edgar away at lunch?

A 25 minutes

B 35 minutes

C 1 hour 15 minutes

D 1 hour 25 minutes

9

Water freezes at 0 °C and 32 °F. Which thermometer shows the temperature at which water freezes?

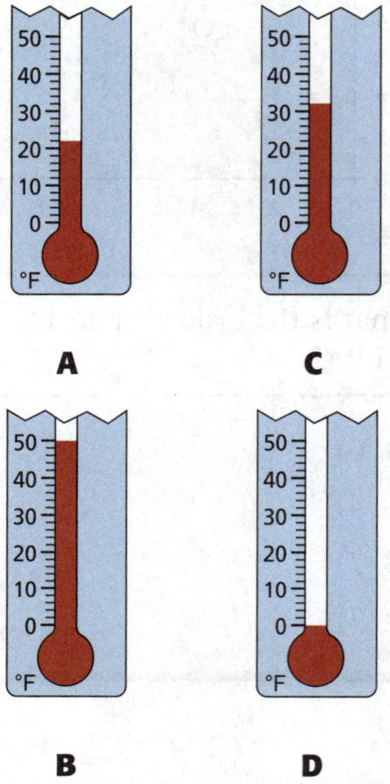

10

Julie completed her math test in 40 minutes. If she started the test at 8:25, what time did she finish?

A 7:45

B 7:55

C 9:05

D 9:15

11

Ana has $1.75 in quarters. How many quarters does Ana have?

A 2

B 3

C 5

D 7

12

Which set of coins has the greatest value?

A

B

C

D

Mathematics Problem Solving

DIRECTIONS ►

Read each question or problem carefully. Then answer the question or work the problem. Mark the space for your answer.

SAMPLE A

What is the value of the 8 in this number?

1853

A 8 ones

B 8 tens

C 8 hundreds

D 8 thousands

SAMPLE B

The table shows the lengths of four U.S. bridges.

Four U.S. Bridges

Name	Length (in meters)
Golden Gate	1280
George Washington	1067
Tacoma Narrows II	853
Mackinac	2626

Which bridge is the *longest*?

A Golden Gate

B George Washington

C Tacoma Narrows II

D Mackinac

1

What is 1265 rounded to the nearest hundred?

A 1200 **C** 1270

B 1260 **D** 1300

2

Tri-County School District has about forty-two thousand students enrolled in kindergarten and all elementary grades. How would that be written as a number?

A 420,000 **C** 4200

B 42,000 **D** 420

3

The Arctic Ocean is 18,456 feet deep at its deepest known point. Which number in 18,456 is in the thousands place?

1	4	6	8
A	**B**	**C**	**D**

4

In 1997, Central City had a population of 54,675. A year later, the population increased by 2000. Which number shows an increase of 2000?

A 74,675

B 56,675

C 52,675

D 34,675

5

Rebecca saw this chart showing the weights in pounds of the five heaviest sharks.

Weights of Sharks

Shark	Weight (in pounds)
Whale shark	46,300
Basking shark	32,000
Great white shark	7300
Greenland shark	2250
Tiger shark	2070

Of the sharks listed, which one's weight is rounded to the nearest *thousand*?

A Whale shark

B Tiger shark

C Great white shark

D Basking shark

6

The chart shows the heights of several students in Jeanne's class.

Heights of Students in Jeanne's Class

Name	Height (in feet and inches)
Bill	4 ft 8 in.
Dave	5 ft 1 in.
Rudy	4 ft 10 in.
Katherine	4 ft 5 in.

Which student is between 4 ft 7 in. and 4 ft 9 in. tall?

A Bill

B Dave

C Rudy

D Katherine

7

Four boys ran 100 meters. Steve ran it in 16.5 seconds. Paul's time was 16.05 seconds. Jim's time was 15.6 seconds, and Gray's time was 15.65 seconds. Who ran the *fastest*?

A Steve

B Paul

C Jim

D Gray

8

In the figure below, each of the triangles is the same size.

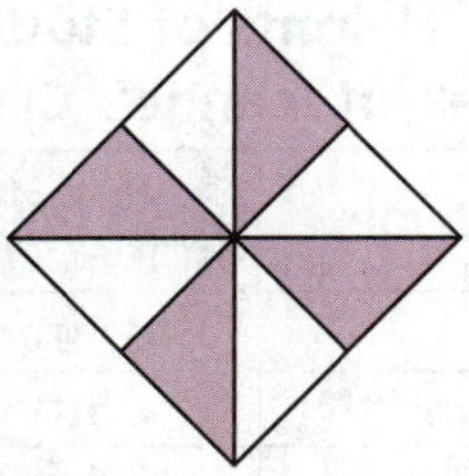

What fractional part of the figure is shaded?

A	B	C	D
$\frac{1}{2}$	$\frac{3}{8}$	$\frac{1}{4}$	$\frac{1}{8}$

9

A game has 65 marbles in it. Each player gets 10 marbles at the beginning of the game. There can be marbles left over. When each player has 10 marbles, what is the greatest number of children who can play the game at one time?

A	B	C	D
10	7	6	5

10

The student council sells candy bars to raise money for new library books. Ian sold $\frac{2}{7}$ of one box, Mindy sold $\frac{2}{7}$ of one box, Chip sold $\frac{3}{7}$ of one box, and Hank sold $\frac{4}{7}$ of one box.

Which two students together sold one box?

A Ian and Mindy

B Mindy and Chip

C Ian and Hank

D Chip and Hank

11

Winn has a dozen cookies to share with some friends.

Which shows the number of people who could share one dozen cookies equally? No cookies will be broken.

A 2, 3, 5, or 6

B 2, 4, 6, or 7

C 2, 3, 4, or 10

D 2, 3, 6, or 12

12

The chart shows the size in acres of lakes in some state parks.

Size of Lakes in Acres

Name of Lake	Number of Acres
Lake Grapevine	7380
Lake Livingston	82,600
Fort Phantom Hill Lake	4236
Lake Corpus Christi	19,336

Which number sentence could be used to find out how many acres larger Lake Livingston is than Fort Phantom Hill Lake?

A $82{,}600 - 4236 = \square$

B $82{,}600 \div 4236 = \square$

C $4236 + 82{,}600 = \square$

D $4236 \div 82{,}600 = \square$

13

Ms. Stein posted this problem on the board.

Problem of the Day

I am a number with the following properties:

I have 2 digits.
My first digit is odd.
The sum of my digits is even.

What number am I?

Which could be the number described in the "Problem of the Day"?

21	34	42	53
A	**B**	**C**	**D**

14

What number goes in the ☐ to make this number sentence true?

$$476 + 0 = \square$$

A 576

B 486

C 477

D 476

15

If $15 + 9 = y$, which of these statements will be true?

A $y + 9 = 15$

B $y - 9 = 15$

C $y \times 9 = 15$

D $y \div 9 = 15$

16

Tony and his father are shopping for a skateboard, helmet, and knee and elbow pads. Tony can spend only $150. The picture shows the price of the skateboard and the helmet Tony plans to buy.

About how much money does Tony have left to spend on knee and elbow pads?

A $20

B $30

C $100

D $120

17

Clay and his friends are in a band. The chart shows the attendance at some of their recent shows.

Attendance

City	Number of People
Atlanta	7525
Chicago	8680
New York City	6470
San Francisco	9519

In how many cities did *at least* 8500 people attend the show?

4	3	2	1
A	**B**	**C**	**D**

18

Dat has twice as many football trading cards as Marty. Marty has 12 fewer cards than Leon. Leon has 28 more cards than Kareem. If Kareem has 32 football trading cards, how many cards does Dat have?

60	72	96	144
A	**B**	**C**	**D**

19

Maria looked up facts on the population of some cities in the South Texas Plains region.

Population of Cities in South Texas Plains

City	Population
Floresville	5868
Goliad	1975
Mission	45,408
Pharr	46,660
Rio Grande City	11,923
Zapata	4856

Which two cities have a population *greater than* 25,000 people?

A Floresville and Zapata

B Mission and Pharr

C Goliad and Rio Grande City

D Rio Grande City and Mission

20

Marcus and Jessie want to know how many fourth-grade students in their school play a team sport. They asked the fourth-grade students and used a tally mark for each student who plays a team sport. Marcus and Jessie used a fast and correct way to find the total number of tally marks.

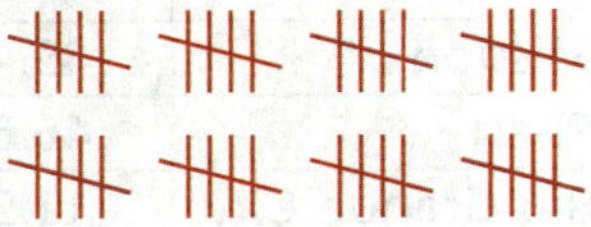

Which method did Marcus and Jessie use?

A 5 + 8

B 8 + 6

C 5 × 8

D 8 × 6

21

Twenty-five students and 4 chaperones went on a class trip to the nature center. The class was given 100 bus tokens to use for the trip. Each person was given two tokens for the bus fare to and from the nature center. How many tokens were *not* used for this trip?

42	50	58	71
A	**B**	**C**	**D**

22

Dwayne worked this problem.

846 × 3

This is how Dwayne worked the problem.

How would Dwayne know he had gotten the wrong answer?

A It should have 5 digits.

B It should be more than 3000.

C It should have 8 as its last digit.

D It should be less than 846.

23

Mahreen is picking out uniforms for her soccer team. Each team member needs a shirt, a pair of shorts, socks, and shoes. Mahreen found a shirt for $10.95, shorts for $8.95, and socks for $3.95. What other information is needed to find the total cost of the uniform?

A The cost of the socks

B The cost of the shirt

C The cost of the shorts

D The cost of the shoes

24

The Dutch Apple Bakery bakes apple pies, cherry pies, and pumpkin pies for Thanksgiving. Orders for 372 apple pies, 176 cherry pies, and 465 pumpkin pies have been placed. *About* how many more apple pies have been ordered than cherry pies for Thanksgiving?

A 100

B 200

C 300

D 400

25

Louis is creating a pattern with flowers in a garden. He starts with 6 red flowers. Then, he makes a row of 8 white flowers, a row of 10 red flowers, and a row of 12 white flowers.

Which operation will Louis use to find the number of white flowers in the next row of white flowers?

A Subtract 4 from the last row of red flowers.

B Add 4 to the last row of white flowers.

C Multiply the number of red flowers in the last row by 4.

D Divide the number of white flowers in the last row by 4.

26

The first figure in the pattern below has four shaded sections.

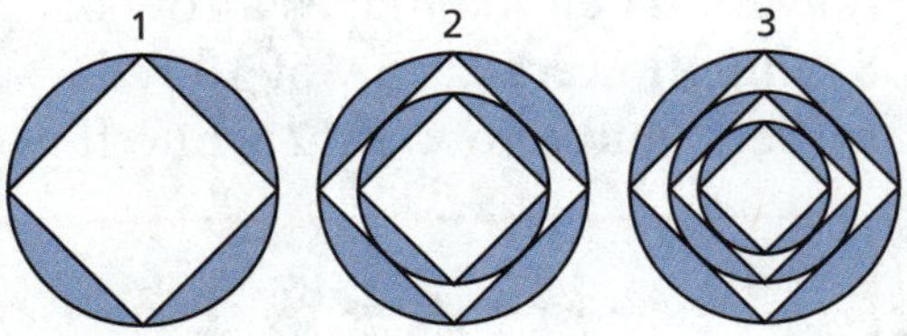

If the pattern continues, how many shaded sections will appear in the fourth figure?

20	16	12	8
A	**B**	**C**	**D**

27

Judy is making a necklace with beads. She is repeating four bead shapes in the same order to make a pattern for the necklace.

If Judy continues the pattern, which bead will be 18th?

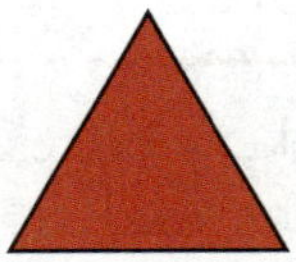

A

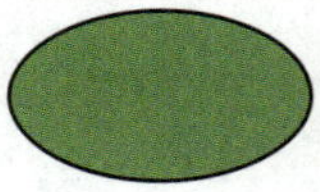

C

B

D

28

Look at the numbers in the chart. Each of the "In" numbers is decreased by the same amount to get the "Out" number.

What's the Amount?

In	Out
5	1
9	5
?	9
19	15

When 9 is the "Out" number, what should the "In" number be?

5	11	13	16
A	**B**	**C**	**D**

29

Etta works at the pool as a lifeguard. She is paid $40 for working a total of 8 hours.

At this rate, how much would Etta get paid for working 40 hours?

A $160

B $200

C $320

D $800

30

If $c - 19 = 45$, what is the value of c?

19	26	45	64
A	**B**	**C**	**D**

31

The chart shows the number of students who have read each book. No student has read more than one book, but 67 students did not read any of these books.

Books Read

Title	Number of Students
Football Heroes	24
The Magician's Helper	14
Easy Meals for Kids to Fix	11
A Trip to the Moon	23

How many more students read one of the books listed than did *not* read any of these books?

5	9	11	13
A	**B**	**C**	**D**

32

Students were asked to name their favorite fruit. This is a graph of their responses.

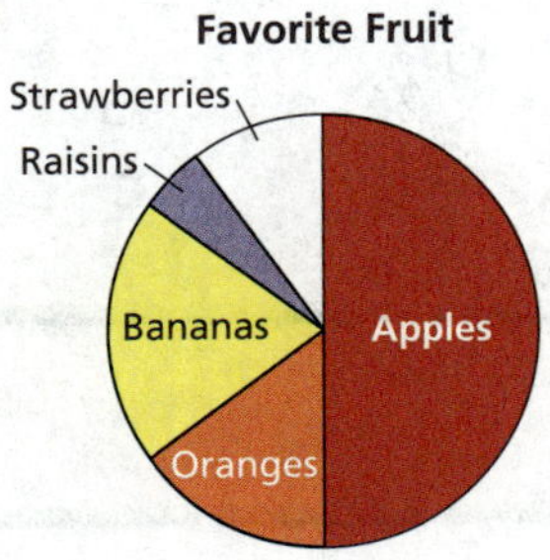

What fruit was the favorite among half of the students?

A Apples
B Oranges
C Bananas
D Strawberries

33

The graph shows the age and number of people riding in a bike race.

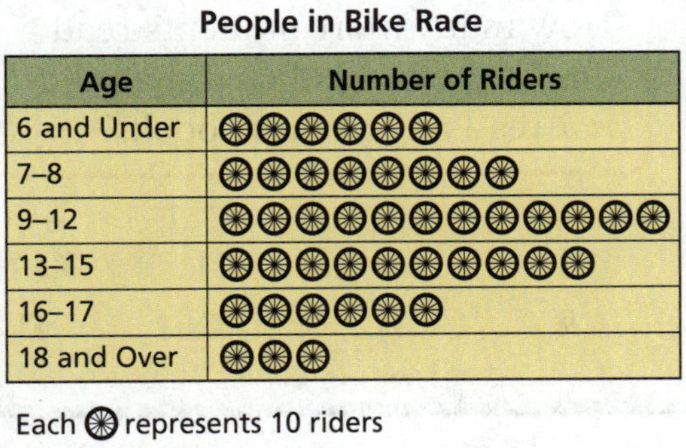

How many more people "6 and Under" rode in the race than people "18 and Over"?

2	3	30	40
A	**B**	**C**	**D**

34

The chart shows instruments played in the school band and the number of students who play each instrument.

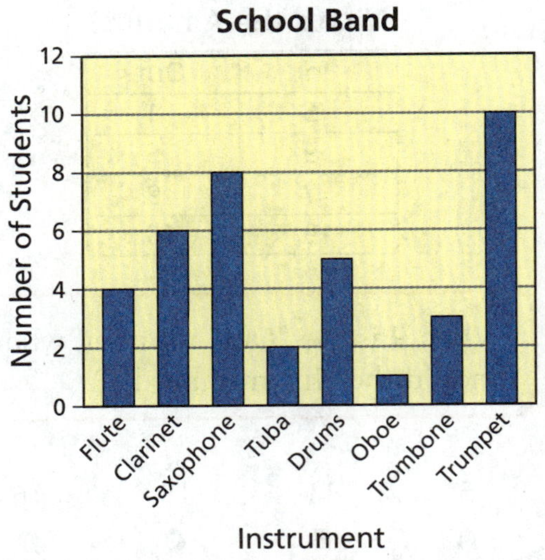

How many instruments are played by *at least* 5 students?

2	3	4	5
A	**B**	**C**	**D**

35

This graph shows the types of pieces in a chess set.

Chess Pieces

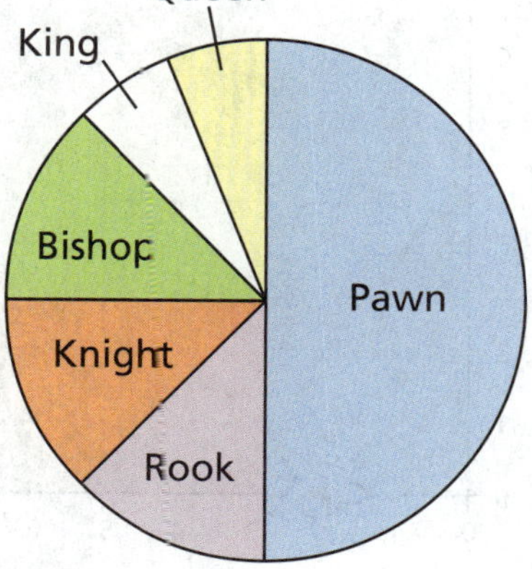

Which three types have an equal number of pieces in a chess set?

A Pawn, Bishop, and Knight

B Knight, Rook, and King

C King, Queen, and Pawn

D Knight, Bishop, and Rook

36

In Camille's drawer, there are three pairs of socks: one red pair, one yellow pair, and one blue pair. She picks two socks at the same time without looking.

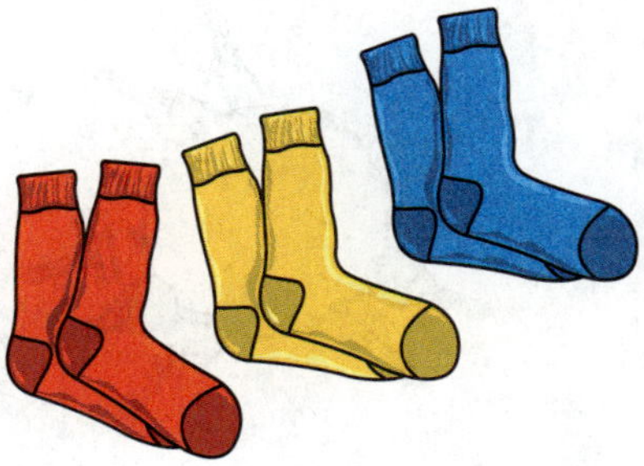

If she reaches into the drawer and picks 2 socks at the same time without looking, which two socks would it be possible for Camille to pick?

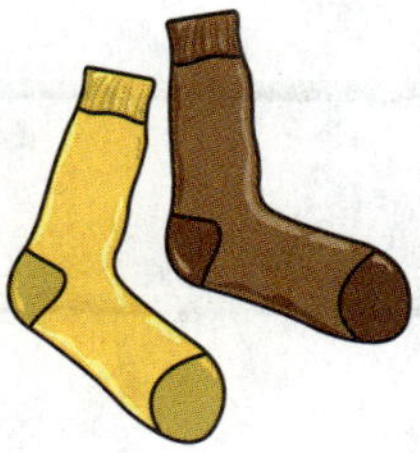

A

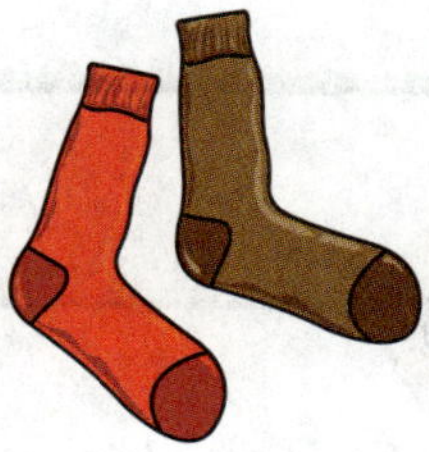

C

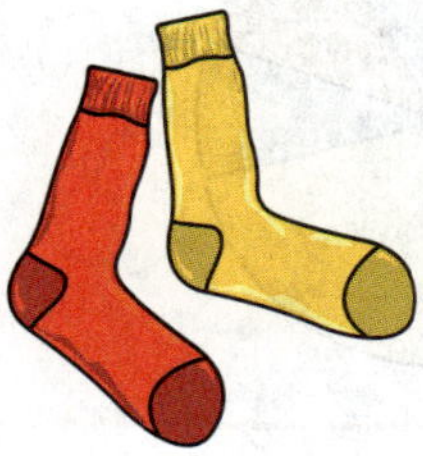

B

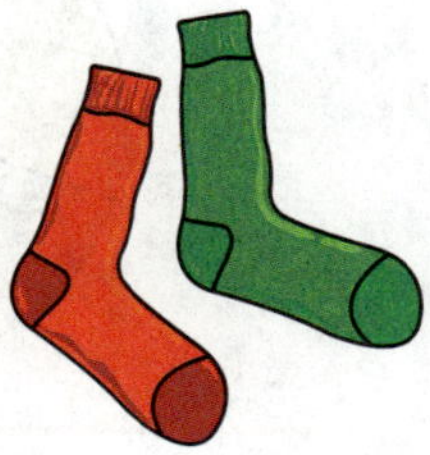

D

37

There are 9 keys on the school janitor's key chain. Two of them are closet keys, three are office keys, and four are classroom keys.

If the janitor picks a key without looking, what is the probability that it will be a classroom key?

$\frac{1}{9}$	$\frac{2}{9}$	$\frac{3}{9}$	$\frac{4}{9}$
A	**B**	**C**	**D**

38

Look at this spinner.

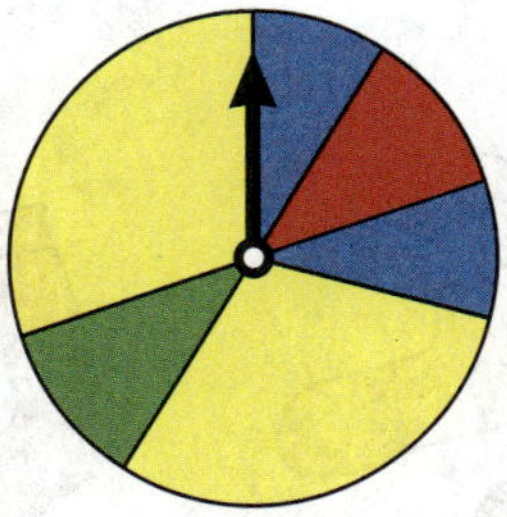

On which color is the arrow *most likely* to land if Ryan spins it once?

A Blue
B Red
C Yellow
D Green

39

Sue and Ray decided to plot the location of the toy store on a grid as part of their math homework.

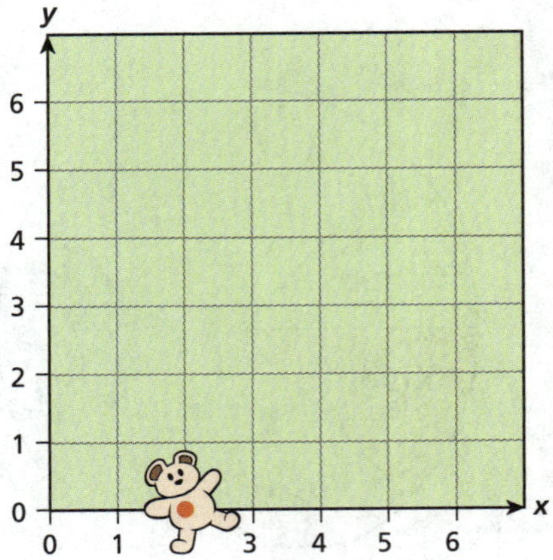

What pair of numbers names the location of the toy store?

(2, 0)	(0, 2)	(2, 1)	(2, 2)
A	**B**	**C**	**D**

40

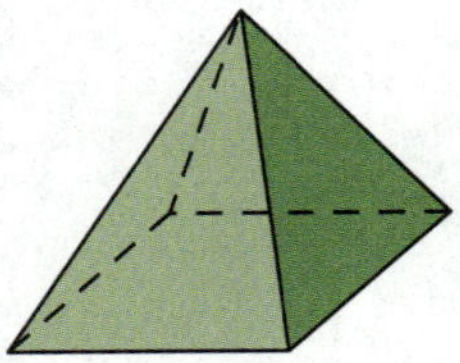

What is the name of the three-dimensional figure pictured above?

A Cone
B Cube
C Triangular pyramid
D Rectangular pyramid

41

This is a view of a garbage container from the side.

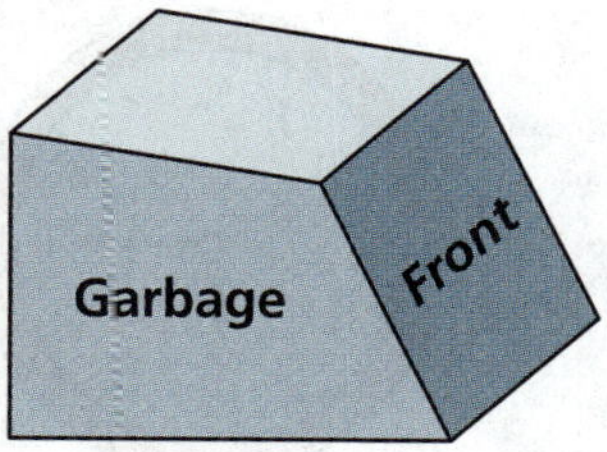

Which picture shows how the container would look if viewed from the front?

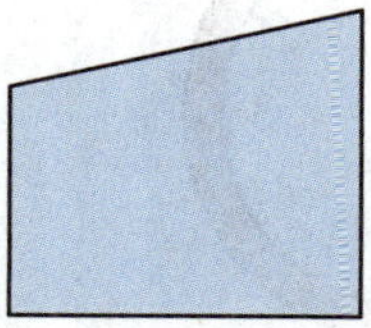

A

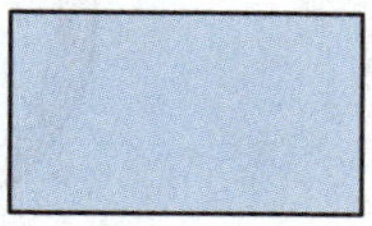

C

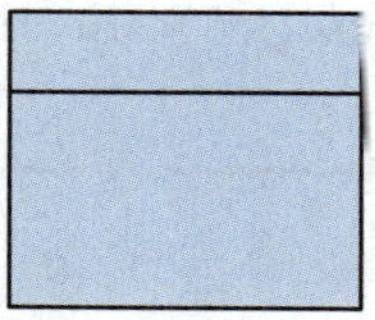

B

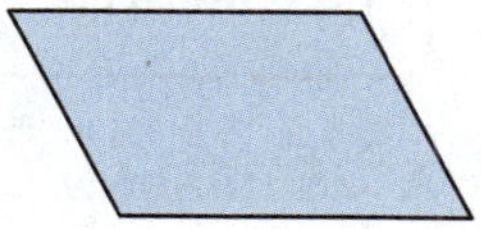

D

42

This is a picture of a bicycle frame. The parts of the frame are labeled.

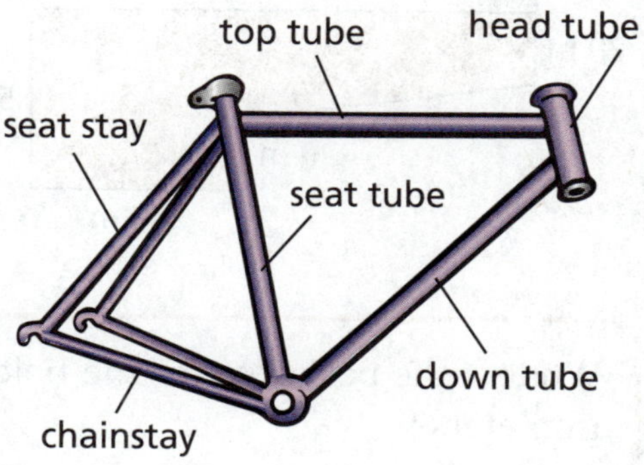

Which part of the frame appears to be parallel to the head tube?

A Top tube

B Seat tube

C Chainstay

D Down tube

43

Saul wants to put a fence around a field on his ranch.

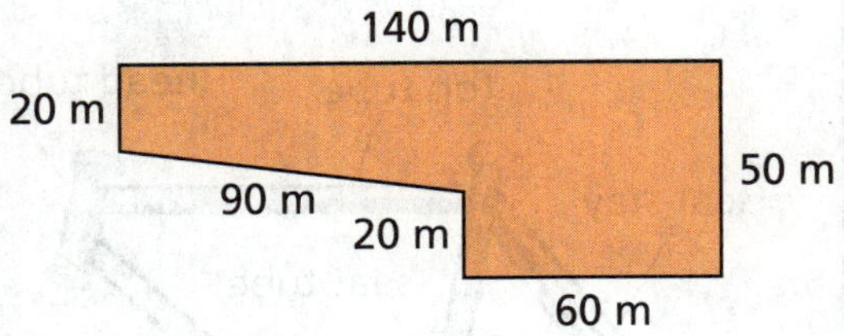

What is the perimeter of the field in meters?

A 200 m

B 360 m

C 380 m

D 480 m

44

Which measure could be the area of a football field?

A 6000 feet

B 6000 inches

C 6000 square miles

D 6000 square meters

45

This is the time that Uri started his homework.

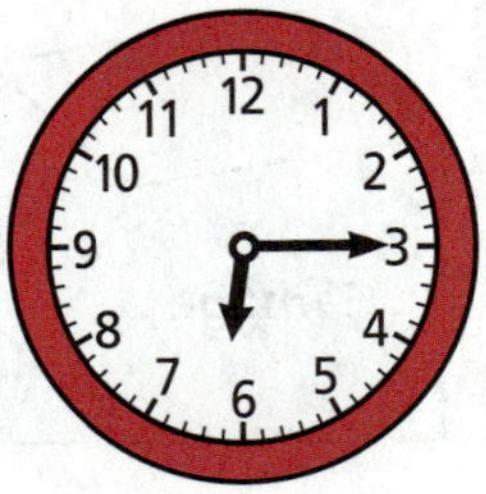

This the time that Uri finished his homework.

How long did it take Uri to do his homework?

A 25 minutes

B 1 hour and 15 minutes

C 1 hour and 25 minutes

D 2 hours and 25 minutes

46

Carrie has four coins worth a total of 37 cents in her wallet. How many *more* pennies does she have than nickels?

A	**B**	**C**	**D**
0	1	2	3

47

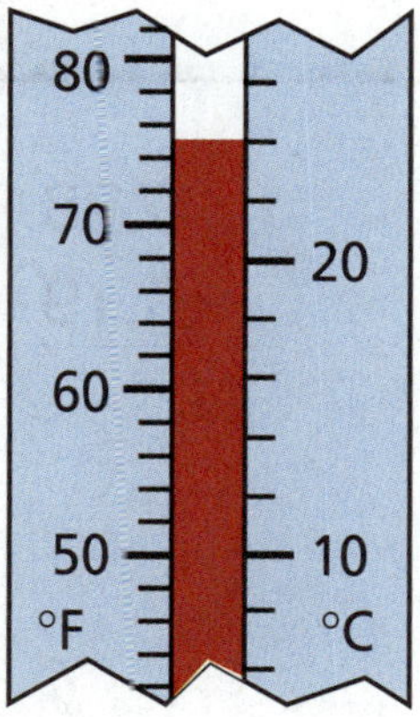

Which temperature is *closest* to the temperature shown on this thermometer in degrees Fahrenheit?

A 25°F

B 35°F

C 75°F

D 85°F

48

Use your inch ruler to help you answer this question.

How many inches long is the leaf from Point A to Point B?

A	**B**	**C**	**D**
$1\frac{1}{2}$ in.	$2\frac{1}{4}$ in.	$2\frac{1}{2}$ in.	$2\frac{2}{3}$ in.

Mathematics Procedures

DIRECTIONS

Read each question or problem carefully. Then answer the question or work the problem. Mark the space for your answer. If a correct answer is *not here*, mark the space for NH.

SAMPLE A

$36 + 21 = \square$

54	55	57	65	NH
A	**B**	**C**	**D**	**E**

SAMPLE B

A painter is painting a large playground. The painter will need 38 gallons of blue paint and 24 gallons of orange paint.

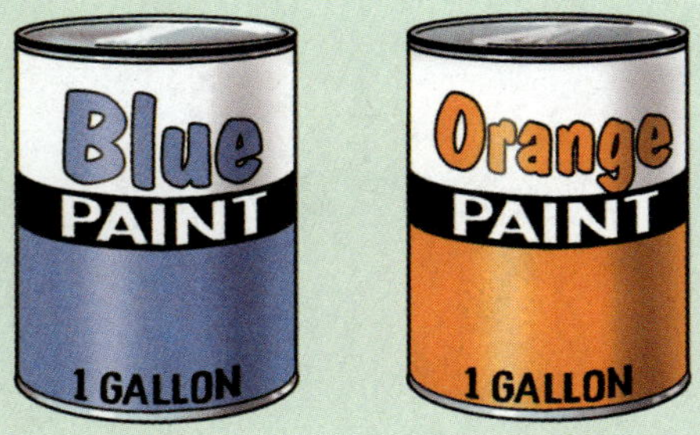

38 Gallons   24 Gallons

How much more blue paint than orange paint will the painter need?

A 10 gallons
B 12 gallons
C 16 gallons
D 18 gallons
E NH

1

$415 - 66 = \square$

349	439	449	451	NH
A	**B**	**C**	**D**	**E**

2

$$\begin{array}{r} 7.28 \\ -\ 3.19 \\ \hline \end{array}$$

A 4.01
B 4.09
C 4.11
D 4.19
E NH

3

$\frac{9}{6} - \frac{8}{6} = \square$

$\frac{1}{6}$	$\frac{2}{6}$	$\frac{3}{6}$	$\frac{4}{6}$	$\frac{5}{6}$
A	**B**	**C**	**D**	**E**

4

$$\begin{array}{r} 663 \\ -\ 278 \\ \hline \end{array}$$

375	395	415	485	NH
A	**B**	**C**	**D**	**E**

5

$$\begin{array}{r} 4693 \\ +\ 428 \\ \hline \end{array}$$

A 4011
B 5011
C 5021
D 5121
E NH

6

$\$2.69 + \$4.79 = \square$

A $6.38
B $6.49
C $7.38
D $7.48
E NH

7

$$\frac{2}{7} + \frac{4}{7} = \square$$

$\frac{6}{14}$	$\frac{24}{14}$	$\frac{6}{7}$	$\frac{7}{7}$	$\frac{24}{7}$
A	**B**	**C**	**D**	**E**

8

$$\begin{array}{r} 6.37 \\ +\ 1.85 \\ \hline \end{array}$$

A 6.12
B 7.12
C 7.22
D 8.22
E NH

9

$$\frac{4}{9} + \frac{1}{9} = \square$$

$\frac{4}{9}$	$\frac{5}{9}$	$\frac{41}{9}$	$\frac{5}{18}$	$\frac{41}{18}$
A	**B**	**C**	**D**	**E**

10

$1.39 + 3.91 = \square$

A 4.20
B 5.20
C 5.29
D 5.30
E NH

11

$84 \div 6 = \square$

12	16	19	21	NH
A	**B**	**C**	**D**	**E**

12

$49 \div 7 = \square$

5	6	7	8	NH
A	**B**	**C**	**D**	**E**

13

$45 \div 8 = \square$

5 R5	6 R3	5	6	NH
A	**B**	**C**	**D**	**E**

14

$$\begin{array}{r} 264 \\ \times \quad 3 \\ \hline \end{array}$$

A 602
B 692
C 697
D 702
E NH

15

$0 \times 5 = \square$

$\frac{1}{5}$	0	1	5	NH
A	**B**	**C**	**D**	**E**

16

$$\begin{array}{r} 27 \\ \times 53 \\ \hline \end{array}$$

A 880
B 1021
C 1080
D 1141
E NH

17

After school, Michael runs laps in soccer practice. He made a chart to show how many yards he ran on Monday, Wednesday, and Friday.

Michael's Results

Day	Yards
Monday	880
Wednesday	1600
Friday	1320

How many yards did Michael run in all?

A 2800 yards

B 3700 yards

C 3710 yards

D 3800 yards

E NH

18

Julie buys a baseball bat for $18.49. The tax is $1.57.

How much does Julie pay for the bat, including tax?

A $19.06

B $19.96

C $20.06

D $20.16

E NH

19

Henry buys two blocks of cheese at the deli. One block weighs 1.18 pounds. The other block weighs 0.67 pound.

How much do the blocks of cheese weigh altogether?

A 1.51 pounds

B 1.56 pounds

C 1.75 pounds

D 1.85 pounds

E NH

20

Evan can lift 173 pounds. Sean can lift 146 pounds.

How many more pounds can Evan lift than Sean?

A 23 pounds

B 27 pounds

C 33 pounds

D 37 pounds

E NH

21

Keiko bought a music CD. The original price was $16.45. The CD was on sale for $2.80 less than the original price. What was the sale price of the CD?

A $13.45

B $13.85

C $14.25

D $14.65

E NH

22

On Saturday, 473 people visited the museum. That number is 168 less than the number of people who visited the museum on Sunday. How many people visited the museum on Sunday?

A 531

B 541

C 561

D 631

E NH

23

In the diving competition, Mindy earned a score of 9.33 on her first dive. She earned a 9.58 on her second dive.

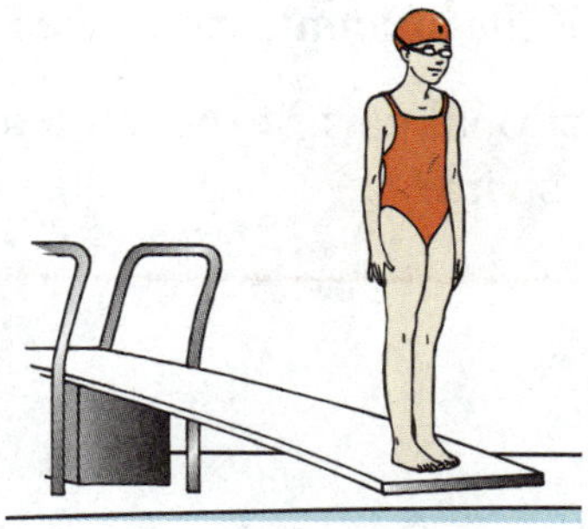

What was Mindy's score for both dives?

A 18.81

B 18.91

C 19.81

D 19.91

E NH

24

Victor went bowling. He knocked down $\frac{3}{5}$ of the pins with the first ball. With his second ball, he knocked down an additional $\frac{1}{5}$ of the original number of pins. What fractional part of the pins did Victor knock down altogether?

$\frac{3}{10}$	$\frac{4}{10}$	$\frac{4}{5}$	$\frac{13}{10}$	$\frac{13}{5}$
A	**B**	**C**	**D**	**E**

25

During gym class, $\frac{2}{6}$ of the students run, $\frac{1}{6}$ of the students swim, and $\frac{3}{6}$ of the students ride bikes. What fractional part of the students do *not* swim?

A	B	C	D	E
$\frac{2}{6}$	$\frac{5}{12}$	$\frac{3}{6}$	$\frac{6}{12}$	$\frac{5}{6}$

26

Don has wrapping paper to sell for the school fundraiser. He has 11 rolls to sell. Don sold $\frac{2}{11}$ of the rolls yesterday. Today, he sold $\frac{5}{11}$ of the rolls of paper.

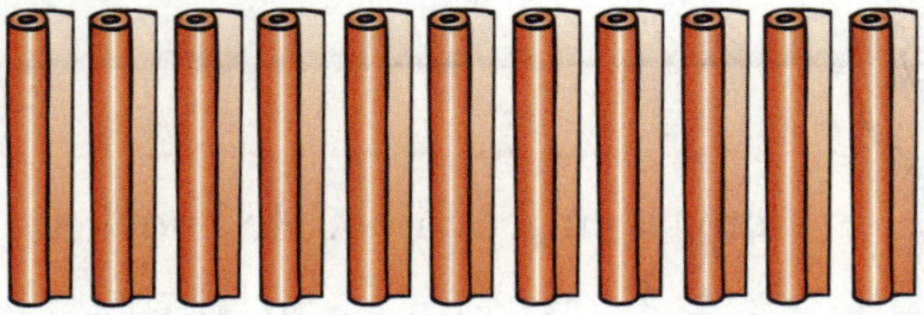

How much greater was the fraction of rolls of wrapping paper Don sold today than the fraction of rolls of wrapping paper he sold yesterday?

A	B	C	D	E
$\frac{3}{22}$	$\frac{2}{11}$	$\frac{3}{11}$	$\frac{7}{22}$	$\frac{7}{11}$

27

Wendy collects postcards. When she went on a trip with her aunt, she bought 3 postcards at each place they visited. If they visited 6 places, how many postcards did Wendy buy altogether?

A	B	C	D	E
13	18	35	36	NH

28

Each weekend, Gordon rides his bike 23 miles delivering newspapers. Last year, he delivered newspapers 46 times.

How many miles did Gordon ride delivering newspapers last year?

A 958 miles

B 978 miles

C 1058 miles

D 1078 miles

E NH

29

The fourth-grade class at Willow Elementary is having a car wash to raise money to buy a class pet. They earn $3.00 for every car they wash.

If the students washed 97 cars, how much money did they earn?

A $100.00

B $280.00

C $291.00

D $301.00

E NH

30

Janelle is having a pizza party for her birthday. Including Janelle, there will be 9 people at the party. Her mother orders 4 pizzas. Each pizza has 8 slices. If each person eats the same number of slices, how many slices are left over?

2	3	4	5	NH
A	**B**	**C**	**D**	**E**

31

Today, the bike racks at Broad Acres Elementary are full.

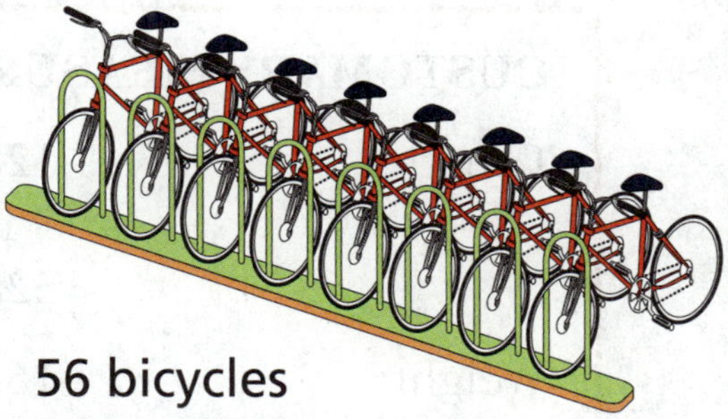

56 bicycles
8 bicycles per rack

Each bike rack holds 8 bicycles. If there are 56 bikes at the school today, how many bike racks does Broad Acres have?

6	7	8	9	NH
A	**B**	**C**	**D**	**E**

32

There are 108 students and 5 teachers in the fifth grade at Hilltop Elementary School. If the principal divides the students into 5 classes, how many classes will have one additional student?

1	2	3	4	NH
A	**B**	**C**	**D**	**E**

Test Best® for the Stanford 10 Reference Sheet
Intermediate 1

CUSTOMARY MEASURES: CONVERSION CHART

Length:	12 inches = 1 foot
	3 feet = 1 yard
	5280 feet = 1 mile
Weight:	16 ounces = 1 pound
Capacity:	8 ounces = 1 cup
	2 cups = 1 pint
	2 pints = 1 quart
	4 quarts = 1 gallon

METRIC MEASURES

Length:	meter
Mass:	gram
Capacity:	liter

TEMPERATURE

Customary Measure — Degrees Fahrenheit (°F)	Water freezes at 32 °F Water boils at 212 °F
Metric Measure — Degrees Celsius (°C)	Water freezes at 0 °C Water boils at 100 °C

Test Best® for the Stanford 10 Reference Sheet
Intermediate 1

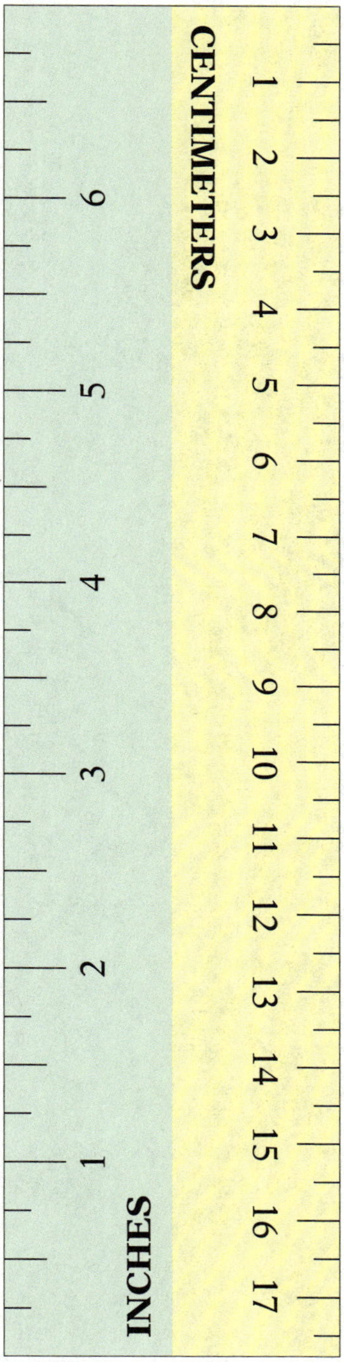